ACT ESSAY WRITING PREP BOOK WITH ESSAY PROMPTS AND SAMPLE ESSAYS

The ACT examination is a registered trademark of ACT Inc, which is neither affiliated with nor endorses this publication.

ACT Essay Writing Prep Book with Essay Prompts and Sample Essays

© COPYRIGHT 2016, 2020. Exam SAM Study Aids & Media

ISBN: 978-1-949282-40-5

All rights reserved. No part of this publication may be reproduced, stored in a retrieval system, or transmitted, in any form or by any means, electronic, mechanical, photocopying, recording, or otherwise, without the prior written permission of the copyright owner.

NOTE: The ACT examination is a registered trademark of ACT Inc, which is neither affiliated with nor endorses this publication.

TABLE OF CONTENTS

Characteristics of the ACT essay	1
ACT Essay Scoring Criteria	2
Information on ACT essay administration	3
Format of ACT essay writing prompts	4
What is an argumentative essay?	5
The "Assertion-Argument-Counterargument-Synthesis-Conclusion" Essay Structure	6
Sample ACT Essay Prompt 1	7
Formulating Your Assertion	8
Writing Your Thesis Statement	9
Supporting and Sustaining Your Argument	11
Acknowledging and Refuting the Counterargument	13
Extending and Elaborating Your Argument	16
Synthesizing the Viewpoints	18
Writing Your Conclusion	19
Sample Essay 1	21
ACT Essays: The Key Points Summed Up	23
Organizing your ACT essay	24
What is argumentative language?	26
Argumentative language exercise	26
Answer to argumentative language exercise	29
Using linking words and phrases effectively in your ACT essay	31
List of Linking Words and Phrases	35
Linking word exercise 1	38
Answers to the linking words exercise	41
ACT Essay Prompt 2	48
Linking word exercise 2	49
Sample Essay 2	52

Using adjectives to assert your opinion	55
Using adjectives – exercise	55
Answers to the adjective exercise	56
Using modality to support your argument	57
Modality exercise	57
Answers to the modality exercise	58
Using qualifiers to strengthen or limit your assertions	59
Qualifiers – exercise	59
Answers to the qualifiers exercise	60
Using verbs in the argument and counterargument	61
Verbs – exercise	61
List of verbs for the argument and counterargument	63
Answers to the verb exercise	65
ACT Essay Prompt 3	66
Sample Essay 3	67
Analysis of essay structure in sample essay 3	70
Analysis of linking words and verbs in sample essay 3	72
Analysis of modality and qualifiers in sample essay 3	75
ACT Essay Prompt 4	78
Sample Essay 4	79
Analysis of essay structure in sample essay 4	82
Analysis of linking words and verbs in sample essay 4	84
Analysis of modality and qualifiers in sample essay 4	87
ACT Essay Prompt 5	90
Sample Essay 5	91
Analysis of essay structure in sample essay 5	94
Analysis of linking words and verbs in sample essay 5	96
Analysis of modality and qualifiers in sample essay 5	99
ACT Essay Prompt 6	102
ACT Essay Prompt 7	103

ACT Essay Prompt 8	104
ACT Essay Prompt 9	105
ACT Essay Prompt 10	106
ACT Essay Prompt 11	107
ACT Essay Prompt 12	108
ACT Essay Prompt 13	109
ACT Essay Prompt 14	110
ACT Essay Prompt 15	111
ACT Essay Prompt 16	112
Appendix – Grammar and Punctuation Review with Exercises	113
Academic Word List	125

Characteristics of the ACT Essay

In order to perform your best on the day of your ACT test, you will need to prepare, and you have already taken steps towards doing that by getting this publication.

So, first of all, you need to know the answers to the following questions: why are you required to write an essay for the ACT test and how do colleges use the essay to assess you as a potential candidate?

You are required to write an essay as part of the ACT because colleges want to see if you have the necessary skills that are required of someone undertaking academic study. These skills include:

- The ability to express your views clearly in writing
- The ability to evaluate and assess problems through logical thinking
- The ability to give reasons and justifications for your point of view
- The ability to anticipate objections to your viewpoints
- The ability to find weaknesses and contradictions in viewpoints that oppose your own
- The ability to synthesize what you see as the pros or cons of various courses of action in order to arrive at an optimal solution
- The ability to conclude or sum up an argument

We will cover each one of these skills in this publication by giving you step-by-step instructions and exercises to help you focus on the nuts and bolts of your argumentative writing.

It is highly recommended that you do the units in this publication in the order that they are given before viewing the sample essays at the end of the book.

Doing the units in this order will help you to assess your strengths and weaknesses more accurately as you work though the material.

Act Essay Scoring Criteria

Your writing will be assessed on how well you fulfill the following criteria:

1. Ideas and Analysis – Stating your own viewpoint and discussing how it relates to at least one other viewpoint
2. Development and Support – Providing detailed reasons and examples to support your views
3. Organization – Organizing your essay clearly
4. Language Use – Communicating your ideas in well-written English, with correct grammar and academic vocabulary

Every essay is scored independently by two different examiners, whose score must be within one point of each other. If not, a third examiner is consulted to resolve the difference.

The essays receive scores from 1 to 6 to in each of the four criteria above by each examiner, and then the score is averaged, for a total possible score of 12. Since the ACT essay is optional, your essay score will not be included in your composite or overall ACT score. However, the essay score will be factored into your Language Arts sub-score.

Note that if you need to improve your grammar or vocabulary skills for the exam, you may wish to look at the grammar rules and exercises, as well as the academic word list, which are provided at the end of this publication.

Information on ACT Essay Administration

On the day of your actual ACT test, you will see three topics on the essay part of the test.

As mentioned previously, the essay part of the ACT is optional. Your college may ask you to take this part of the test.

You will be given 40 minutes to write your essay.

You will write your essay in pencil on the answer paper provided.

Mechanical pencils are not permitted.

Since longer, well-developed essays generally receive higher scores, we recommend that the length for your essay should be from 500 to 600 words.

Format of ACT Essay Writing Prompts

For the ACT essay, you will see a writing prompt, which consists of a particular debatable issue, and then three differing perspectives on that issue.

You will need to read the issue and perspectives carefully and then provide your own viewpoint on the issue in your essay.

When describing how your view relates to another perspective, you can agree in whole or in part, or you can provide a completely different viewpoint.

Your essay will need to state your viewpoint clearly and analyze how your perspective relates to at least one of the other perspectives provided in the prompt.

Student sometimes worry about which perspective examiners would prefer. However, your score will not be affected by the opinions you state, but rather on the quality of your writing.

It is also important to note that factual accuracy is not considered in the ACT essay, so you can create facts or statistics to support your argument. You are required to argue a perspective and compare your viewpoint to other perspectives on the essay, so as long as your so-called facts support your opinion, it doesn't matter if they are actually true or not.

Bear these considerations in mind as you work through the examples in this study guide, and of course, remember them for the day of your exam as well.

We will provide sample essays and prompts throughout this study guide.

What is an argumentative essay?

An argumentative essay requires a student to take a position on a contentious topic and state a clear viewpoint on it.

Since all of the prompts on the ACT essay writing test are on debatable issues, you will need to write an argumentative essay for the ACT.

The argumentative essay consists of the following four or five paragraphs:

- Assertion – This is provided in the first paragraph, where you concisely state your viewpoint.

- Argument – In the second paragraph, you need to argue your perspective. This means that you give reasons and examples that support your position on the issue

- Counterargument – This is normally given in the third paragraph. In the counterargument, you need to acknowledge and analyze at least one other perspective on the topic.

- Synthesis – In the synthesis, you need to analyze how your position relates to at least one other position provided in the essay prompt. The synthesis can be provided in paragraph four or combined with the counterargument in paragraph three.

- Conclusion – In the last paragraph of the essay, you restate your assertions and sum up. The conclusion can also have a forward-looking aspect.

We will describe each of the above parts of the essay in the following units of this book.

Assertion-Argument-Counterargument-Synthesis-Conclusion

As mentioned previously, the components of an argumentative essay are:

- Assertion

- Argument

- Counterargument

- Synthesis

- Conclusion

In this unit, we give definitions and explanations for the above concepts, discussing each one of these components in turn.

In the next unit, we discuss alternative ways to organize these components in your ACT essay, depending upon the line of argument you decide to put forward.

Sample ACT Essay Prompt 1

As we work through each section of a sample ACT essay in the first part of this study guide, we will consider the following essay prompt:

When the automobile was invented, it was hailed as a revolutionary device that would afford us with more convenience and freedom in our daily lives. With developments in automotive transport, we are now able to travel and work like never before. It has been reported that 95 percent of all American households now own at least one vehicle. Yet, are the problems caused by this increase in vehicular traffic worth the convenience vehicles give us? With the prevalence of automotive usage around the world today, one must take pause to consider the implications associated with this issue.

Perspective One

We are now so accustomed to using vehicles for our daily lives that any attempt to control our usage of them would be ineffective. Each individual driver should be free to decide when and how to use his or her vehicle.

Perspective Two

The amount of air pollution and potential health problems caused by the exhaust from cars and other vehicles has become unbearable. The government must create new, strict laws in order to control all vehicle usage.

Perspective Three

The government should put some controls in place for vehicle usage, because it leads to pollution and sedentary lifestyles. While there are many rules and regulations that already limit our freedoms, certain controls on vehicle use are needed.

Formulating Your Assertion

Once you have read the essay prompt and decided on which viewpoint you are going to take, you need to begin to develop your assertion.

In general, an assertion is a statement of your point of view on a particular problem or topic. In your essay, you should normally make your primary assertion in the first paragraph. Your primary assertion should be a clear statement that responds to the specific point raised in the essay question.

You will notice that the essay question itself is already an assertion and the perspectives provide three additional viewpoints, so you need to first think about the pros and cons of the situation before formulating your own primary assertion.

You can formulate your primary assertion by following these steps:

1. What are the advantages of the topic under discussion? In this case, the advantages of non-motorized transport include, among other things, the reduction of pollution, as well as health benefits to the general population, because people will walk and cycle more frequently.

2. Now think about the potential disadvantages. The general public often complain of excessive governmental control in their daily lives. The idea that the government over-regulates day-to-day behaviors that should be left to common sense is an issue that needs to be addressed.

3. Finally, form a primary assertion for paragraph 1. Your primary assertion should indicate that you have an awareness that there is contention surrounding your position.

Remember that the first sentence of your ACT essay needs to introduce your topic in a general way. You should put your primary assertion after the introductory sentence. So, a possible first paragraph for the above essay topic is as follows:

> There is a constant question in society nowadays about the environmental and health risks caused by the use of motorized vehicles. In spite of public complaints about the excessive involvement of the government in our private lives, it is irrefutable that increasing regulatory measures by a certain amount would bring about benefits to society.

Writing Your Thesis Statement

You can also add a thesis statement at the end of your introductory paragraph. A thesis statement indicates how your essay is organized and gives a preview of the position you are going to take on the topic. Thesis statements often begin with the phrases "This essay will discuss…" or "I will show that…."

In reality, though, a thesis statement is not strictly necessary for ACT essays because you will have already indicated your position in your primary assertion sentence. In the above example, the writer's position is that his or her proposal "would bring about benefits to society."

If you prefer to add a thesis statement to your ACT essay, the first paragraph would look something like this:

> There is a constant question in society nowadays about the environmental and health risks caused by the use of motorized vehicles. In spite of public complaints about the excessive involvement of the government in our private lives, it is irrefutable that increasing regulatory measures by a certain amount would bring about benefits to society. This essay will discuss the supporters and detractors to

governmental involvement in the realm of traffic control, before describing two measures that the government might take to address the issue.

So, in the paragraph above, the thesis statement is as follows:
> This essay will discuss the supporters and detractors to governmental involvement in the realm of traffic control, before describing two measures that the government might take to address the issue.

Before moving on to the next section, we would be remiss if we did not point out that you will, of course, make many other assertions in your essay when you provide your supporting points.

However, remember that your essay will be the most effective when you begin with a strong statement of your overall position in your primary assertion in the first paragraph.

Supporting and Sustaining Your Argument

In an ACT essay, an argument is when you provide reasons and examples to support your position.

- Remember that the essence of a good argument is that it gives persuasive and convincing reasons and examples to support its logical development.
- In other words, you need to provide valid points that logically support your position.
- You need to express your argument in a sustained and reasoned way, effectively using the argumentative language that is provided in one of the subsequent units in this material.
- In the subsequent units, we will also show you how to use other words and phrases to express and strengthen certain assertions that you make in your argument.
- You should note that, at times, you may need to limit your assertions, depending upon the strength and validity of other views.

Now let's look again at the first paragraph to the essay:

There is a constant question in society nowadays about the environmental and health risks caused by the use of motorized vehicles. In spite of public complaints about the excessive involvement of the government in our private lives, it is irrefutable that increasing regulatory measures by a certain amount would bring about benefits to society.

Because the primary assertion in the above paragraph is that increasing regulatory measures by a certain amount would bring about benefits to society, your argument should continue in the second paragraph by giving reasons for and examples of the benefits that will be derived from such a measure.

By continuing with the discussion of benefits, you ensure that your argument has a good flow.

Achieving good flow will make your essay more persuasive and will also make it easier to read.

Now recall the advantages that we came up with when preparing our primary assertion. The advantages to governmental involvement in traffic control were:

1. The reduction of pollution
2. Health benefits to the general population because of more frequent walking and cycling.

Then decide which one of these advantages has more strength, in your opinion.

Remember that an argument will be stronger when you can give evidence or examples to support it.

In this essay, we will use the health argument in the second paragraph, giving evidence from Denmark.

Here is a possible second paragraph for our essay topic:

> There is no doubt that countries using non-motorized transport as a norm have a better level of health in the general population. In Denmark, where most people cycle to work, it is reported that levels of heart disease and stroke are far lower than they are in other countries.

You can see that by backing up your assertion with a concrete example, like the one about Denmark above, you give your assertion more support.

Acknowledging and Refuting the Counterargument

A counterargument is an objection or disadvantage to your proposed course of action.

- Just as with your argument, you will need to give reasons and examples to support the counterargument in order to demonstrate that you appreciate the validity of perspectives that differ to your own.
- If you do not do this, your essay might appear too simple or limited.
- When you express the counterargument, it will be beneficial to state it indirectly, using argumentative language.
- Using argumentative language will show that you understand the strength of other perspectives, while distancing yourself from the other viewpoint.

For your convenience, we provide the second paragraph of the essay again below:

> There is no doubt that countries using non-motorized transport as a norm have a better level of health in the general population. In Denmark, where most people cycle to work, it is reported that levels of heart disease and stroke are far lower than they are in other countries.

Notice that, up to this point, the second paragraph has spoken in support of your primary assertion, which is that "increasing regulatory measures by a certain amount would bring about benefits to society." Now we have to address the drawbacks to your primary assertion.

Recall the disadvantages that we mentioned when preparing our primary assertion. The disadvantages to governmental involvement in traffic control were:

1. The general public often complain of too much governmental control in their lives.

2. The government over-regulates day-to-day behaviors that should be left to common sense.

Bearing in mind these disadvantages, here is one possible way to continue the second paragraph of our essay:

> In spite of the health benefits, some would argue that cycling as a means of transport must be a matter left to personal choice. We constantly hear objections from the public about policies that cause unnecessary governmental intervention and bureaucracy in our lives. They claim the choice of whether or not to use an environmentally-friendly form of transport should be a matter of individual conscience. But we only have to consider the rising levels of environmental damage around the world to understand that personal choice and individual conscience as a means to improving the environment have, in fact, been ineffective thus far.

Notice the argumentative language ("some would argue that…" and "They claim") in the first and third sentences. These phrases help to identify this response as a viewpoint that opposes your own.

You also place a distance between your own viewpoint and other perspectives because you clearly identify the other side as "some" and "they."

In addition to using argumentative language, you will normally come to some sort of resolution after you state the other viewpoint. Notice how the other viewpoint in the second paragraph is resolved by the final sentence:

> But we only have to consider the rising levels of environmental damage around the world to understand that personal choice and individual conscience as a means to improving the environment have, in fact, been ineffective thus far.

Such a resolution provides a good transition into the next paragraph of your essay and also serves to improve the flow or line of your writing.

Extending and Elaborating Your Argument

It is essential to understand that it will not be sufficient to give only one argument in your essay.

On a practical level, your essay should be around 500 words at a minimum, and it would be difficult to achieve that length without giving a second argument.

More significantly, if you do not give a second argument and an elaboration of that second argument, your essay and your thinking will appear underdeveloped.

So, the next step is to think about how to extend your argument or line of reasoning in paragraph 3.

In the final part of paragraph 2, we talked about the opposing view that there should be an element of personal choice in deciding to use alternative forms of transport. In essence, this belief in personal choice is the cornerstone of the opposing view.

So, in the next part of the essay, we need to think about how to further advance our argument and cast doubt on other perspectives. In our sample essay on traffic control, we can cast doubt on opposing views by finding flaws with the aspect of personal choice.

Think about countries where inhabitants do not always have the luxury of personally choosing to use an automobile, such remote villages. Then cite examples of countries where personal choice has led to excessive petrol consumption, such as in the United States.

Having planned our line of reasoning, here is a possible second argument for the third paragraph for our essay:

> We only need to look at remote villages that do not have automotive traffic to see how negatively motorized vehicles have affected other areas of our planet. One

can see that levels of air pollution and other forms of environmental contamination are far less in these villages than in so-called "developed" countries. Consider the converse case, for instance, in the United States, where a heavy reliance on motor vehicles has resulted in this country being one of the largest emitters of greenhouse gases in the world.

Note that it is not strictly necessary to attempt to refute your second argument by providing another counterargument. In fact, sometimes giving another counterargument at this point would weaken your position.

In the example above, we provide the second argument about remote villages. We then elaborate and strengthen that argument by citing a further example in the United States. We also elaborate rather than counter-argue at this point because the idea of rising pollution levels was already mentioned in paragraph 2.

While this sample essay has two main arguments, please note that it is likely that you may even need to have a third argument in your essay in order to elaborate your ideas fully.

Synthesizing the Viewpoints

In your ACT essay, your synthesis is where you continue to acknowledge other perspectives, while showing that your primary assertion and arguments hold more sway than other perspectives.

- A synthesis can simply consist of a strong reiteration of your primary assertion and the reasons why it still rings true.
- A synthesis can sometimes involve arriving at some sort of compromise between the other viewpoints.
- If you are going to offer a compromise, you need to state the specific conditions of it in your synthesis.

The following synthesis for our example essay includes a proposed compromise:

> Therefore, it is evident that a compromise needs to be reached in order to balance the limitations on personal freedom that can result from imposing governmental control over the issue, on the one hand, while addressing the very exigent concerns of cleaning up the world's environment and promoting healthy habits amongst its inhabitants, on the other. After all, it is often stated that personal freedom of choice is the cornerstone of any democratic society.

Notice that the synthesis above uses the key words "compromise" and "in order to balance" to indicate clearly that a compromise is being proposed.

The balancing of other viewpoints is also signaled by the phrases "on the one hand" and "on the other."

Writing Your Conclusion

The conclusion to your ACT essay consists of your final comments, which need to indicate the proposition that you are putting forward in response to the issue at hand. In other words, your conclusion needs to state the specific conditions of the outcome that you are proposing.

- You may need to re-state your position in your conclusion.
- Your conclusion is normally placed directly after the synthesis.
- The conclusion is often in the same paragraph as your synthesis.
- You may offer solutions to the issue at hand in your conclusion.
- Most importantly: Don't be noncommittal. Take a stand.
- Your essay will be viewed poorly if you say that both views have merit in general, but then you fail to state precisely what outcome you are advocating.
- In other words, avoid making a concluding remark such as: "As you can see, there are pros and cons to both arguments, so it is difficult to find a resolution."

The following conclusion for our example essay puts forward two possible solutions:

Perhaps the best solution to the issue at hand is to have the government provide certain incentives to those who decide not to use motorized vehicles. For instance, the government could offer rebates or subsidies on bicycle purchases. Another possible course of action would be to introduce certain governmental controls, but to establish those controls within very clear limits. Alternating car use by vehicle registration number has been an effective solution in certain countries. Under this scheme, car owners with odd-numbered registrations can use their vehicles on certain days of the week, while owners of vehicles with registrations ending in an even number are permitted to use their vehicles only on the other days. Violating this policy would result in fines or other sanctions. To sum up, one thing is clear: whether by positive reinforcement, as in the first example, or by negative reinforcement as in the second, both remedies take into account the pressing concern of the state of the global environment, as well as protecting the need of the population for both personal health and individual freedom.

In the example above, two possible courses of action are put forward: one is an incentive plan, and the other is a plan involving fines and sanctions.

Notice how both courses of action are described precisely and with sufficient detail. Closing your essay in this way leaves a positive impact on the person who is reading and evaluating it.

Sample Essay 1

We reproduce the entire example essay in full here so that you can see how the parts relate to each other and how it achieves a good line of argument.

There is a constant question in society nowadays about the environmental and health risks caused by the use of motorized vehicles. In spite of public complaints about the excessive involvement of the government in our private lives, it is irrefutable that increasing regulatory measures by a certain amount would bring about benefits to society. This essay will discuss the supporters and detractors to governmental involvement in the realm of traffic control, before describing two measures that the government might take to address the issue.

There is no doubt that countries using non-motorized transport as a norm have a better level of health in the general population. In Denmark, where most people cycle to work, it is reported that levels of heart disease and stroke are far lower than they are in other countries. In spite of the health benefits, some would argue that cycling as a means of transport must be a matter left to personal choice. We constantly hear objections from the public about policies that cause unnecessary governmental intervention and bureaucracy in our lives. They claim the choice of whether or not to use an environmentally-friendly form of transport should be a matter of individual conscience. But we only have to consider the rising levels of environmental damage around the world to understand that personal choice and individual conscience as a means to improving the environment have, in fact, been ineffective thus far.

We only need to look at remote villages that do not have automotive traffic to see how negatively motorized vehicles have affected other areas of our planet. One can see that levels of air pollution and other forms of environmental contamination are far less in these villages than in so-called "developed" countries. Consider the converse case, for instance, in the United States, where a heavy reliance on motor vehicles has resulted in this country being one of the largest emitters of greenhouse gases in the world.

Therefore, it is evident that a compromise needs to be reached in order to balance the limitations on personal freedom that can result from imposing governmental control over the issue, on the one hand, while addressing the very exigent concerns of cleaning up the world's environment and promoting healthy habits amongst its inhabitants, on the other. After all, it is often stated that personal freedom of choice is the cornerstone of any democratic society. Perhaps the best solution to the issue at hand is to have the government provide certain incentives to those who decide not to use motorized vehicles. For instance, the government could offer rebates or subsidies on bicycle purchases.

Another possible course of action would be to introduce certain governmental controls, but to establish those controls within very clear limits. Alternating car use by vehicle registration number has been an effective solution in certain countries. Under this scheme, car owners with odd-numbered registrations can use their vehicles on certain days of the week, while owners of vehicles with registrations ending in an even number are permitted to use their vehicles only on the other days. Violating this policy would result in fines or other sanctions. To sum up, one thing is clear: whether by positive reinforcement, as in the first example, or by negative reinforcement as in the second, both remedies take into account the pressing concern of the state of the global environment, as well as protecting the need of the population for both personal health and individual freedom. [580 words]

ACT Essays:
The Key Points Summed Up

So, to sum up our discussion, here is a brief list of key points to bear in mind when writing your ACT essay.

How to argue your point:

- Answer the question with a primary assertion

- Provide a sustained line of argument

- Give evidence or examples to support it

- Address arguments which contradict your own line of argument

- Demonstrate a clear and convincing synthesis and conclusion to give a resolution to the essay and to take a stand

Organizing Your ACT Essay

We know that an ACT essay contains the following elements: Assertion, Argument, Counterargument, Synthesis, and Conclusion. However, you may have some doubt regarding how these individual elements should be organized.

While the organization of your essay can vary depending on your writing skill and technique, as well as the essay theme, we believe that there are two particular organization schemes for the ACT essay which are especially effective. They are as follows:

Scheme 1

- Assertion

- Argument 1

- Counterargument

- Argument 2

- Elaboration

- Synthesis

- Conclusion

A scheme 1 organizational style was used in the sample essay on non-motorized vehicles given in the previous section. When considering the amount and strength of existing counterarguments, however, it may be more beneficial in some cases to use the scheme 2 organizational style.

Scheme 2

- Assertion
- Argument 1
- Counterargument 1
- Argument 2
- Counterargument 2
- Synthesis
- Conclusion

As stated previously, it may be necessary in some cases to give more than two arguments and counterarguments; the above guidelines are offered by way of general advice on structure and organization.

We provide an example of an essay written using scheme 2 in sample essay 2 in this publication, which is on the theme of tourism.

What is Argumentative Language?

In certain of the previous units in this publication, we have touched on the notion of "argumentative language."

"Argumentative language" means the words and phrases that you can use to introduce your own assertions and elaborations on those assertions.

You can also use argumentative language to introduce and distance yourself from other viewpoints.

Let's look at the argumentative language used in paragraph 1 of sample essay 1:

<u>There is a constant question</u> in society nowadays about the environmental and health risks caused by the use of motorized vehicles. In spite of public complaints about the excessive involvement of the government in our private lives, <u>it is irrefutable that</u> increasing regulatory measures <u>by a certain amount</u> would bring about benefits to society. This essay will discuss the supporters and detractors to this assertion, before describing two measures that the government might take to address the issue.

Exercise: *Now look at the reminder of sample essay 1 and underline the argumentative language. Please do not underline linking words (for example, because, in spite of, etc.) because we will analyze those in a later unit.*

The answer is provided on the pages immediately following this exercise.

There is no doubt that countries using non-motorized transport as a norm have a better level of health in the general population. In Denmark, where most people cycle to work, it is reported that levels of heart disease and stroke are far lower than they are in other countries. In spite of the health benefits, some would argue that cycling as a means of transport must be a matter left to personal choice. We constantly hear objections from the public about policies that cause unnecessary governmental intervention and bureaucracy in our lives. They claim the choice of whether or not to use an environmentally-friendly form of transport should be a matter of individual conscience. But we only have to consider the rising levels of environmental damage around the world to understand that personal choice and individual conscience as a means to improving the environment have, in fact, been ineffective thus far.

We only need to look at remote villages that do not have automotive traffic to see how negatively motorized vehicles have affected other areas of our planet. One can see that levels of air pollution and other forms of environmental contamination are far less in these villages than in so-called "developed" countries. Consider the converse case, for instance, in the United States, where a heavy reliance on motor vehicles has resulted in this country being one of the largest emitters of greenhouse gases in the world.

Therefore, it is evident that a compromise needs to be reached in order to balance the limitations on personal freedom that can result from imposing governmental control over the issue, on the one hand, while addressing the very exigent concerns of cleaning up the world's environment and promoting healthy habits amongst its inhabitants, on the other. After all, it is often stated that personal freedom of choice is the cornerstone of any democratic society. Perhaps the best solution to the issue at hand is to have the government provide certain incentives to those who decide not to use motorized vehicles. For instance, the government could offer rebates or subsidies on bicycle purchases.

Another possible course of action would be to introduce certain governmental controls, but to establish those controls within very clear limits. Alternating car use by vehicle registration number has been an effective solution in certain countries. Under this scheme, car owners with odd-numbered registrations can use their vehicles on certain days of the week, while owners of vehicles with registrations ending in an even number are only permitted to use their vehicles on the other days. Violating this policy would result in fines or other sanctions. To sum up, one thing is clear: whether by positive reinforcement, as in the first example, or by negative reinforcement as in the second, both remedies take into account the pressing concern of the state of the global environment, as well as protecting the need of the population for both personal health and individual freedom.

Answer to Argumentative Language Exercise

There is no doubt that countries using non-motorized transport as a norm have a better level of health in the general population. In Denmark, where most people cycle to work, it is reported that levels of heart disease and stroke are far lower than they are in other countries. In spite of the health benefits, some would argue that cycling as a means of transport must be a matter left to personal choice. We constantly hear objections from the public about policies that cause unnecessary governmental intervention and bureaucracy in our lives. They claim, the choice of whether or not to use an environmentally-friendly form of transport should be a matter of individual conscience. But we only have to consider the rising levels of environmental damage around the world to understand that personal choice and individual conscience as a means to improving the environment have, in fact, been ineffective thus far.

We only need to look at remote villages that do not have automotive traffic to see how negatively motorized vehicles have affected other areas of our planet. One can see that levels of air pollution and other forms of environmental contamination are far less in these villages than in so-called "developed" countries. Consider the converse case, for instance, in the United States, a heavy reliance on motor vehicles has resulted in this country being one of the largest emitters of greenhouse gases in the world. Therefore, it is evident that a compromise needs to be reached in order to balance the limitations on personal freedom that can result from imposing governmental control over the issue, on the one hand, while addressing the very exigent concerns of cleaning up the world's environment and promoting healthy habits amongst its inhabitants, on the other. After all, it is often stated that personal freedom of choice is the cornerstone of any democratic society. Perhaps the best solution to the issue at hand is to have the government provide certain incentives to those who decide not to use motorized vehicles. For instance, the government could offer rebates or subsidies on bicycle purchases.

<u>Another possible course of action would be to</u> introduce certain governmental controls, but to establish those controls within very clear limits. Alternating car use by vehicle registration number has been an effective solution in certain countries. Under this scheme, car owners with odd-numbered registrations can use their vehicles on certain days of the week, while owners of vehicles with registrations ending in an even number are only permitted to use their vehicles on the other days. Violating this policy would result in fines or other sanctions. <u>To sum up</u>, <u>one thing is clear</u>: whether by positive reinforcement, as in the first example, or by negative reinforcement as in the second, <u>both remedies take into account</u> the pressing concern of the state of the global environment, as well as protecting the need of the population for both personal health and individual freedom.

Please notice that, depending on how you structure your essay, certain of the phrases above may be used to support your assertions, and alternatively the same phrases could be used to distance yourself from another perspective on the issue. It's a matter of how cautious and diplomatic you want to be.

If the above exercise was a struggle for you, we recommend that you make a list of the above phrases and commit then to memory in order to use some of them in your essay on the day of your actual ACT exam.

Using Linking Words and Phrases Effectively in Your ACT Essay

The effective use of linking words and phrases will make your ACT essay more organized, more persuasive, and easier to read.

Unfortunately, problems can occur with punctuation and word placement when using linking words and phrases. Of course, in order to make the best impact with your ACT essay, you should be sure to observe the conventions of correct grammar and punctuation.

Linking words and phrases (also known as discursive markers) fall into three categories. Please read the following rules for word placement and punctuation for each category:

Connectives – Linking Words and Subordination

Sentence linking words can help you combine short sentences together to create more complex sentence structures.

Sentence linking words and phrases fall into three categories:

- sentence linkers
- phrase linkers
- subordinators

In order to understand how to use these types of sentence linking words and phrases correctly, you will need to know some basics of English grammar.

Please study the examples below carefully before you do the exercises.

SENTENCE LINKERS

Sentence linkers are used to link two complete sentences together.

A complete sentence is one that has a grammatical subject and a verb.

Sentence linkers are usually placed at the beginning of a sentence and are followed by a comma.

They can also be preceded by a semicolon and followed by a comma when joining two sentences together. When doing so, the first letter of the first word of the second sentence must not be capitalized.

Now look at the following examples.

Sentence linker examples:

>You need to enjoy your time at college. *However*, you should still study hard.

>You need to enjoy your time at college; *however*, you should still study hard.

In the examples above, the grammatical subject of the first sentence is "you" and the verb is "need to enjoy."

In the second sentence, "you" is the grammatical subject and "should study" is the verb.

PHRASE LINKERS

In order to understand the difference between phrase linkers and sentence linkers, you must first be able to distinguish a sentence from a phrase.

A phrase linker must be followed by a phrase, while a sentence linker must be followed by a sentence.

Remember that a phrase does not have both a grammatical subject and a verb, while sentences contain grammatical subjects and verbs.

Here are some examples of phrases:

- her beauty and grace
- life's little problems
- a lovely summer day in the month of June
- working hard
- being desperate for money

Note that the last two phrases above use the –ing form, known in these instances as the present participle.

Present participle phrases, which are often used to modify nouns or pronouns, are sometimes placed at the beginning of sentences as introductory phrases.

Here are some examples of sentences:

    Mary worked all day long.

    My sister lives in Seattle.

    Wintertime is brutal in Montana.

"Mary," "my sister," and "wintertime" are the grammatical subjects of the above sentences.

Remember that verbs are words that show action or states of being, so "worked," "lives," and "is" are the verbs in the three sentences above.

Look at the examples that follow:

    Phrase linker example 1 – no comma: He received a promotion *because of* his dedication to the job.

"His dedication to the job" is a noun phrase.

    Phrase linker example 2 – with comma: Because of his dedication to the job, he received a promotion.

When the sentence begins with the phrase linker, we classify the sentence as an inverted sentence.

Notice that you will need to place a comma between the two parts of the sentence when it is inverted.

SUBORDINATORS

Subordinators must be followed by an independent clause. Subordinators cannot be followed by a phrase.

The two clauses of a subordinated sentence must be separated by a comma.

The structure of independent clauses is similar to that of sentences because independent clauses contain a grammatical subject and a verb.

Subordinator examples:

> *Although* he worked hard, he failed to make his business profitable.
>
> He failed to make his business profitable, *although* he worked hard.

There are two clauses: "He worked hard" and "he failed to make his business profitable." The grammatical subjects in each clause are the words "he", while the verbs are "worked" and "failed."

Now look at the linking words and phrases on the following pages. Note which ones are sentence linkers, which ones are phrase linkers, and which ones are subordinators. Then refer to the rules above to remember the grammatical principles for sentence linkers, phrase linkers, and subordinators.

Sentence linkers for additional information

further

furthermore

apart from this

what is more

in addition

additionally

in the same way

moreover

Sentence linkers for giving examples

for example

for instance

in this case

in particular

more precisely

namely

in brief

in short

Sentence linkers for stating the obvious

obviously

clearly

naturally

of course

surely

after all

simply

quite simply

Sentence linkers for giving conclusions

finally

to conclude

lastly

in conclusion

Sentence linkers for giving generalizations

in general

on the whole

as a rule

as often happens

as often as not

for the most part

generally speaking

in most cases

to the best of my knowledge

Sentence linkers for stating causes and effects

thus

accordingly

hence

therefore

in that case

under those circumstances

as a result

for this reason

as a consequence

consequently

in effect

Sentence linkers for concession or unexpected results

however

nevertheless

meanwhile

Sentence linkers for contrast

on the other hand

on the contrary

alternatively

rather

Sentence linkers for paraphrasing or restating

in other words

that is to say

that is

Sentence linkers for similarity

similarly

in the same way

likewise

Phrase linkers for giving additional information

besides

in addition to

Phrase linkers for stating causes and effects

because of

due to

owing to

Phrase linkers for contrast

in contrast to

instead of

rather than

without

Phrase linkers for concession or unexpected results

but for

despite

in spite of

Phrase linkers for comparison

compared to

like

Subordinators

although

as

as much as

because

but

due to the fact that

even though

however much

in so much as

not only . . . but also

once

since

so

so that

unless

until

when

whereas

while

Time words that are both phrase linkers and subordinators

after

before

<u>Special cases</u>

yet – "yet" can be used as both a subordinator and as a sentence linker.

in order to – "in order to" must be followed by the base form of the verb.

thereby – "thereby" must be followed by the present participle.

Now try the exercises on the next page.

Exercise 1 – Using Linking Words as Connectives

Look at the sets of sentences in the exercises below. Make new sentences, using the phrase linkers, sentence linkers, and subordinators provided. In many cases, you will need to create one single sentence from the sentences provided. You may need to change or delete some of the words in the original sentences. Be careful with capitalization and punctuation in your answers. The answers are provided on the pages after the exercise.

1) The temperature was quite high yesterday. It really didn't feel that hot outside.

   a) In spite of . . .

   b) The temperature . . . nevertheless . . .

2) Our star athlete didn't receive a gold medal in the Olympics. He had trained for competition for several years in advance.

   a) Our star athlete . . . although . . .

   b) Despite . . .

3) There are acrimonious relationships within our extended family. Our immediate family decided to go away on vacation during the holiday season to avoid these conflicts.

   a) Because of . . .

   b) Because . . .

   c) Due to the fact that . . .

4) My best friend had been feeling extremely sick for several days. She refused to see the doctor.

a) My best friend . . . however . . .

b) My best friend . . . but . . .

5) He generally doesn't like drinking alcohol. He will do so on social occasions.

a) While . . .

b) He generally . . . yet . . .

6) The government's policies failed to stimulate spending and expand economic growth. The country slipped further into recession.

a) The government's policies . . . thus . . .

b) The government's policies . . . so . . .

7) Students may attend certain classes without fulfilling a prerequisite. Students are advised of the benefit of taking at least one non-required introductory course.

a) Even though . . .

b) Students may attend . . . apart from this . . .

8) There have been advances in technology and medical science. Infant mortality rates have declined substantially in recent years.

a) Owing to . . .

b) Since . . .

9) It was the most expensive restaurant in town. It had rude staff and provided the worst service.

a) It was the most . . . besides

b) In addition to . . .

10) *Now combine these three sentences.*

The judge did not punish the criminal justly. He decided to grant a lenient sentence. He did not send out a message to deter potential offenders in the future.

a) Instead of . . . and thereby . . .

b) Rather than . . . in order to . . .

Before you attempt your answer for question 10, look for the cause and effect relationships among the three sentences.

Answers to Linking Words Exercise

Question 1

Answer (1a):

a) In spite of the temperature being quite high yesterday, it really didn't feel that hot outside.

The words "in spite of" are a phrase linker, not a sentence linker, so they take a phrase, not a clause.

The verb "was" needs to be changed to "being" in order to form a present participle phrase.

Answer (1b):

There are two possible answers:

b) The temperature was quite high yesterday. Nevertheless, it really didn't feel that hot outside.

b) The temperature was quite high yesterday; nevertheless, it really didn't feel that hot outside.

"Nevertheless" is a sentence linker. As such, it can be used to begin a new sentence. Alternatively, the semicolon can be used to join the original sentences. If the semicolon is used, the first letter of the word following it must not be capitalized.

Question 2:

Answer (2a):

a) Our star athlete didn't receive a gold medal in the Olympics, although he had trained for competition for several years in advance.

"Although" is a subordinator, so the two sentences can be combined without any changes.

Answer (2b):

b) Despite having trained for competition for several years in advance, our star athlete didn't receive a gold medal in the Olympics.

The two parts of the sentence are inverted, and the verb "had" needs to be changed to "having" to make the present participle form.

Question 3:

Answer (3a):

a) Because of acrimonious relationships within our extended family, our immediate family decided to go away on vacation during the holiday season to avoid these conflicts.

"Because of" is a phrase linker. As such, the subject and verb (there are) need to be removed from the original sentence in order to form a phrase.

Answer (3b):

b) Because there are acrimonious relationships within our extended family, our immediate family decided to go away on vacation during the holiday season to avoid these conflicts.

Answer (3c):

c) Due to the fact that there are acrimonious relationships within our extended family, our immediate family decided to go away on vacation during the holiday season to avoid these conflicts.

"Because" and "due to the fact that" are subordinators, so no changes to the original sentences are required.

The phrase "to avoid these conflicts" can be omitted since this idea is already implied by the words "acrimonious relationships."

Question 4:

Answer (4a):

There are two possible answers.

a) My best friend had been feeling extremely sick for several days. However, she refused to see the doctor.

a) My best friend had been feeling extremely sick for several days; however, she refused to see the doctor.

Answer (4b):

b) My best friend had been feeling extremely sick for several days, but she refused to see the doctor.

"But" is a subordinator, so the two sentences can be combined without any changes.

Question 5:

Answer (5a):

a) While he generally doesn't like drinking alcohol, he will do so on social occasions.

Answer (5b):

"Yet" can be used as both a subordinator and as a sentence linker, so there are three possible answers in this instance.

b) He doesn't like drinking alcohol. Yet, he will do so on social occasions.

b) He doesn't like drinking alcohol; yet, he will do so on social occasions.

b) He doesn't like drinking alcohol, yet he will do so on social occasions.

The difference is that the third sentence places slightly less emphasis on the particular occasions in which he will drink than the other two sentences.

Question 6:

Answer (6a):

"Thus" is a sentence linker, so there are two possible answers:

a) The government's policies failed to stimulate spending and expand economic growth. Thus, the country slipped further into recession.

a) The government's policies failed to stimulate spending and expand economic growth; thus, the country slipped further into recession.

Answer (6b):

b) The government's policies failed to stimulate spending and expand economic growth, so the country slipped further into recession.

"So" is a subordinator. The two sentences may therefore be joined without any changes.

Question 7:

Answer (7a):

There are two possible answers.

a) Even though students may attend certain classes without fulfilling a prerequisite, they are advised of the benefit of taking at least one non-required introductory course.

a) Even though students are advised of the benefit of taking at least one non-required introductory course, they may attend certain classes without fulfilling a prerequisite.

"Even though" is a subordinator, so no changes are needed. It is advisable to change the word "students" to the pronoun "they" on the second part of the new sentence in order to avoid repetition.

The order or the clauses may be changed in the new sentence since there is no cause and effect relationship between the two original sentences.

Answer (7b):

There are two possible answers:

b) Students may attend certain classes without fulfilling a prerequisite. Apart from this, they are advised of the benefit of taking at least one non-required introductory course.

b) Students may attend certain classes without fulfilling a prerequisite; apart from this, they are advised of the benefit of taking at least one non-required introductory course.

"Apart from this" is a sentence linker, so it needs to be used at the beginning of a separate sentence.

Question 8:

Answer (8a):

a) Owing to advances in technology and medical science, infant mortality rates have declined substantially in recent years.

"Owing to" is a phrase linker that shows cause and effect. The cause is advances in technology and medical science, and the effect or result is the decline in infant mortality rates.

Since "owing to" is a phrase linker, the grammatical subject of the original sentence (there) and the verb (have been) are removed when creating the new sentence.

Answer (8b):

b) Since there have been advances in technology and medical science, infant mortality rates have declined substantially in recent years.

"Since" is a subordinator, so you can combine the sentences without making any changes.

Remember to use a comma between the two parts of the sentence.

Question 9:

Answer (9a):

a) It was the most expensive restaurant in town, besides having rude staff and providing the worst service.

"Besides" is a phrase linker, so use the present participle form of both verbs in the second original sentence. Accordingly, "had" becomes "having" and "provide" becomes "providing."

Answer (9b):

There are two possible answers.

b) In addition to being the most expensive restaurant in town, it had rude staff and provided the worst service.

b) In addition to having rude staff and providing the worst service, it was the most expensive restaurant in town.

"In addition to" is a phrase linker, so the present participle forms are used in the phrase containing this word.

The order of the original sentences can be changed since there is no cause and effect relationship between these ideas.

Question 10:

Answer (10a):

a) Instead of punishing the criminal justly and thereby sending out a message to deter potential offenders in the future, the judge decided to grant a lenient sentence.

Answer (10b):

b) Rather than punishing the criminal justly in order to send out a message to deter potential offenders in the future, the judge decided to grant a lenient sentence.

"Instead of" and "rather than" need to be used with the present particle form (punishing).

"Thereby" must be followed by the present participle form (sending).

However, "in order to" needs to take the base form of the verb (send).

ACT Essay Prompt 2

Now look at the essay prompt and perspectives below. Then try the exercise on the next page.

With people in many parts of the world working extended working hours, vacations seem to have taken on greater importance recently. Vacation time helps us get away and shores us up for the return to the stresses in our individual lives. Since travel is becoming increasingly affordable, people are now even traveling to far-flung "exotic" destinations that they might not have been able to visit previously. However, does this travel bring benefits or burdens to the destinations that tourist visit? Since there has been a rise in travel to places that were previously considered untouched, this issue is worthy of analysis.

Perspective 1

People spend money abroad when they travel, which improves foreign economies. The foreign economy should pay for any problems caused by tourism from the income generated by tourists. Travelers should therefore be allowed to go wherever they want.

Perspective 2

People should be more responsible about international travel. Flying abroad should only be permitted if the traveler is doing something that will benefit the foreign destination, such as working as a volunteer.

Perspective 3

When people travel to so-called exotic venues, they are really traveling so some of the poorest countries in the world. This results in untold burdens on foreign communities and economies, as well as over-stretching their health, policing, and legal systems.

Exercise: Now read the sample essay that follows and place the linking words or phrases provided below into the correct gaps. When you have finished, compare your answers to those in sample essay 2.

for instance / hence / although / because / because of / not only /
but also / yet / further / first of all / even though / nevertheless /
in addition / however

Cheaper flights are making it more and more affordable and convenient for people around the world to travel to other countries. In the US alone, there has been a recent proliferation in low-cost and budget airlines, which has made it easier for the average family to afford a holiday to some "exotic" destination. _____ , in many cases, "exotic" may mean one of the less economically well-off countries of the world. Sometimes having less infrastructure and being removed from the hustle and bustle of the traveler's normal life, these destinations are selected because they are seen as holding a restorative balm to modern life's daily stresses. _____ such vacations may be beneficial for the traveler, the negative effects of the increasing throngs of tourists on the poorer countries of the world should give us reason to take pause _____ it is clear that there are problems associated with the expanding global tourism industry.

Apart from the obvious environmental damage that tourism causes, _____ , we must consider increasing crime rates. Some local residents might see tourists as easy prey because, _____ are they in unfamiliar territory and therefore less able to take care of themselves, _____ because they carry visible items of wealth such as jewelry and electronic equipment, which can be readily resold for a quick profit. _____, travelers might argue in response to this claim that they know how to protect themselves, so there is no danger. Some might even claim that they leave all valuables home when traveling abroad. _____, such arguments focus merely on theft, without taking in account other crimes. _____, some people will knowingly purchase illegal copies of movies from a store abroad that sells pirated copies of digital goods. Believing that the authorities turn a blind eye to such "soft" crimes, normally law-abiding tourists behave in this way because they realize that they can do so with impunity. Consider the even more extreme case of tourists who go abroad to take advantage of that country's lack of enforcement of recreational drug use or prostitution. _____ recreational drugs and prostitution are illegal in certain of these countries, some tourists again believe that they can justify their actions merely because of the fact that they will escape punishment. _____, these tourists fail to consider that these crimes are not enforced because of the country's economic conditions in the first place, and that by participating in these crimes, they are exacerbating and perpetuating crime even further in the host country.

_____, another major problem is healthcare. With greater mobility comes greater danger of spreading contagious diseases. On a local level, tourists' illnesses, accidents and injuries place a strain on local healthcare systems and in extreme cases can threaten the lives of the local people who are unaccustomed to certain strains of diseases. Travelers might claim that they would not consider traveling when they are under the weather. _____, others might argue that they never travel without getting a medical insurance policy for their trips. Nevertheless, the flaws in these arguments can easily be revealed: people can carry strains of bacteria-causing illnesses without feeling unwell, and regardless of whether one is in possession of a medical insurance policy or not, he or she might require a stay in a local hospital _____ the illness or injury, thereby putting further strain on local resources.

These are just two reasons why tourism can do more harm than good. These phenomena suggest that one should devote careful awareness to his or her selection of a tourist destination by taking into consideration the effects of one's proposed trip on the host country. All in all, it might appear that "voluntourism" and "ecotourism" will become more popular in the future if the general public takes the needs of the host country into account when deciding where to go on holiday.

Sample Essay 2

Cheaper flights are making it more and more affordable and convenient for people around the world to travel to other countries. In the US alone, there has been a recent proliferation in low-cost and budget airlines, which has made it easier for the average family to afford a holiday to some "exotic" destination. <u>However</u>, in many cases, "exotic" may mean one of the less economically well-off countries of the world. Sometimes having less infrastructure and being removed from the hustle and bustle of the traveler's normal life, these destinations are selected because they are seen as holding a restorative balm to modern life's daily stresses. <u>Although</u> such vacations may be beneficial for the traveler, the negative effects of the increasing throngs of tourists on the poorer countries of the world should give us reason to take pause <u>because</u> it is clear that there are problems associated with the expanding global tourism industry.

Apart from the obvious environmental damage that tourism causes, <u>first of all</u>, we must consider increasing crime rates. Some local residents might see tourists as easy prey because, <u>not only</u> are they in unfamiliar territory and therefore less able to take care of themselves, <u>but also</u> because they carry visible items of wealth such as jewelry and electronic equipment, which can be readily resold for a quick profit. <u>Nevertheless</u>, travelers might argue in response to this claim that they know how to protect themselves, so there is no danger. Some might even claim that they leave all valuables home when traveling abroad. <u>Yet</u>, such arguments focus merely on theft, without taking in account other crimes. <u>For instance</u>, some people will knowingly purchase illegal copies of movies from a store abroad that sells pirated copies of digital goods. Believing that the authorities turn a blind eye to such "soft" crimes, normally law-abiding tourists behave in this way because they realize that they can do so with impunity. Consider the even more extreme case of tourists who go abroad to take advantage of that country's lack of enforcement of recreational drug use or prostitution. Even though recreational drugs and prostitution are illegal in certain of these countries, some tourists again believe that they can justify their actions merely because of the fact that they will escape punishment. Hence, these tourists fail to consider that these crimes are not enforced because of the country's economic conditions in the first place, and that by participating in these crimes, they are exacerbating and perpetuating crime even further in the host country.

In addition, another major problem is healthcare. With greater mobility comes greater danger of spreading contagious diseases. On a local level, tourists' illnesses, accidents and injuries place a strain on local healthcare systems and in extreme cases can threaten the lives of the local people who are unaccustomed to certain strains of diseases. Travelers might claim that they would not consider traveling when they are under the weather. Further, others might argue that they never travel without getting a medical insurance policy for their trips. Nevertheless, the flaws in these arguments can easily be revealed: people can carry strains of bacteria-causing illnesses without feeling unwell, and regardless of whether one is in possession of a medical insurance policy or not, he or she might require a stay in a local hospital because of the illness or injury, thereby putting further strain on local resources.

These are just two reasons why tourism can do more harm than good. These phenomena suggest that one should devote careful awareness to his or her selection of a tourist destination by taking into consideration the effects of one's proposed trip on the host country. All in all, it might appear that "voluntourism" and "ecotourism" will become more popular in the future if the general public takes the needs of the host country into account when deciding where to go on holiday. [633 words]

Please note that you can interchange positions of the following words:

However / Nevertheless / Yet

Although / Even though

In addition / Further

Using Adjectives to Assert Your Opinion

Adjectives are words that are used to describe nouns. You should use adjectives in your ACT essay to strengthen and intensify your assertions, as well as to weaken or limit perspectives that are different than yours

- Remember that a noun can normally be classified as a person, place, or thing.
- For example, in the sentence "Science is a boring subject" the word "boring" is an adjective and the word "subject" is a thing.

Now look at these two sentences:

The present rate of global warming is a problem in the world today.

The present rate of global warming is an exigent problem in the world today.

The second sentence is much more persuasive than the first because it uses the adjective "exigent" to emphasize that the problem is extremely urgent or pressing.

Exercise: Look at the following sentences and underline the adjectives that the writer uses to advance her assertions. Then make a mental note of these adjectives so that you can use them in your ACT essay. The answers are provided on the following page.

1) Our history is the nation's greatest asset.

2) The landscape is an integral part of our identity.

3) Our heritage is fundamental to our culture.

4) Accepting change is a critical part of making decisions.

5) This decision is of paramount importance.

6) Historical buildings are a key part of our culture.

7) Clear policies on this issue are essential.

Answers to the Adjective Exercise

1) Our history is the nation's <u>greatest</u> asset.

2) The landscape is an <u>integral</u> part of our identity.

3) Our heritage is <u>fundamental</u> to our culture.

4) Accepting change is a <u>critical</u> part of making decisions.

5) This decision is of <u>paramount</u> importance.

6) Historical buildings are a <u>key</u> part of our culture.

7) <u>Clear</u> policies on this issue are <u>essential</u>.

Using Modality to Support Your Argument

When we talk about "modality" in a grammatical sense, we are referring to the use of modal verbs in writing.

- Modal verbs include the following: can, could, may, must, ought to, shall, should, would, have to
- Modal verbs are extremely useful in ACT essays because they can be used to help express your assertions and strengthen your examples.
- Modal verbs can also be used to limit the intensity of the other viewpoint.
- Remember that you can use modal verbs in either the affirmative or negative form.
- For example, "should" is the affirmative form, while "should not" is the negative form.

Exercise: *Place the correct modal verb in the sentences below from the options provided at the end of each sentence. Notice that in some sentences, both options are correct. When both options are correct, please state which option strengthens the assertion the most. The answers are provided on the following page.*

1) We _____ not hide our heritage. (should / have to)

2) We do not _____ look far to encounter this phenomenon. (have to / must)

3) We _____ not make that decision arbitrarily. (must / should)

4) We _____ work together to achieve this aim. (shall / could)

5) We _____ protect the environment. (would / ought to)

Answers to Modality Exercise

1) We _____ not hide our heritage. (should / have to)

   The correct answer is "should."

   In order to use "have to," the word order would be different: We do not have to hide our heritage.

2) We do not _____ look far to encounter this phenomenon. (have to / must)

   The correct answer is "have to." Must is incorrect grammatically.

3) We _____ not make that decision arbitrarily. (must / should)

   Both answers are correct. "Must" is stronger than "should" in this case because it is used to expresses a strong obligation, rather than a recommendation.

4) We _____ work together to achieve this aim. (shall / could)

   Both answers are correct. "Shall" is stronger than "could" because it expresses a future intention, rather than a mere possibility.

5) We _____ protect the environment. (would / ought to)

   The correct answer is "ought to." "Would" does not provide the correct sense to the sentence.

Using Qualifiers to Strengthen or Limit Your Assertions

"Qualify" means limit or modify, particularly to modify the meaning of a word or phrase. Qualifiers are words that can be used in your ACT essay either to make your assertions sound more serious or to advance your own arguments.

- Qualifiers can also be used to acknowledge other perspectives.
- Qualifiers often include words that can be used as adverbs, such as: surely, fairly, allegedly
- Remember that, to make a very broad grammatical generalization, adverbs often end with the letters –ly.

Exercise: *Imagine that you are writing an argumentative essay that puts forward your argument that the government's economic policies and proposals are largely ineffectual. Please underline the qualifier in each sentence. Then state whether the qualifier is being used to advance your own argument or whether the qualifier is being used to acknowledge another perspective.*

1) Admittedly, the government's plans have some redeeming features.
2) This economic policy has been rightly criticized.
3) There are certainly advantages to this economic proposal.
4) Equally there are arguments against the proposal.
5) However, policy and reality are often mutually exclusive.

Answers to the Qualifiers Exercise

1) <u>Admittedly</u>, the government's plans have some redeeming features.

You will recall that your argument is that the government's economic policies and proposals are largely ineffectual. So, the qualifier in the sentence above is being used to acknowledge another perspective.

2) This economic policy has been <u>rightly</u> criticized.
Used to advance your own argument

3) There are <u>certainly</u> advantages to this economic proposal.

Used to acknowledge another perspective

4) <u>Equally</u> there are arguments against the proposal.

Used to advance your own argument

5) However, policy and reality are often <u>mutually</u> exclusive.

Used to advance your own argument

Using Verbs in the Argument and Counterargument

As stated previously in our discussion of linking words and phrases, verbs are words that show action. Practice how to use verbs to your advantage in your ACT essay by completing the exercise below.

Exercise: Sample essay 2 was an argumentative essay analyzing whether tourism brings more harm than good to the poorer counties of the world. Some sentences from that essay are reproduced below. Look at the list of useful argumentative verbs and verb phrases on the page following the exercise. Then read the sentences below and underline all of the argumentative verb forms in each sentence. Note that you should not identify every verb, but rather only the argumentative ones. The answers to the exercises are given on the page following the verb list.

1) Nevertheless, travelers might argue in response to this claim that they know how to protect themselves, so there is no danger.

2) Some might even claim that they leave all valuables home when traveling abroad.

3) Yet, such arguments focus merely on theft, without taking in account other crimes.

4) Believing that the authorities turn a blind eye to such "soft" crimes, normally law-abiding tourists behave in this way because they realize that they can do so with impunity.

5) Consider the even more extreme case of tourists who go abroad to take advantage of that country's lack of enforcement of recreational drug use or prostitution.

6) Even though recreational drugs and prostitution are illegal in certain of these countries, some tourists again believe that they can justify their actions merely because of the fact that they will escape punishment.

7) Hence, these tourists fail to consider that these crimes are not enforced because of the country's economic conditions in the first place, and that by participating in these crimes, they are exacerbating and perpetuating crime even further in the host country.

Useful Verbs for the Argument and Counterargument

address

afford (meaning: provide)

agree

approach

argue

assert

assume

believe

challenge

claim

coerce

comment

conclude

consider

concede

contend

contradict

convince

demonstrate

deny

disagree

discern

dispute

emphasize

enumerate

exacerbate

hasten

hold / hold the view

imply

infer

influence

maintain

perpetrate

perpetuate

persuade

peruse

point out

ponder

propose

protect

qualify

query

question

realize

recognize

recommend

refute

reject

remark

report

repudiate

reveal

say

state

suggest

sum up

stipulate

take heed

take into account

view

value

warn

Answers to the Verb Exercise

1) Nevertheless, travelers might <u>argue</u> in response to this claim that they know how to protect themselves, so there is no danger.

2) Some might even <u>claim</u> that they leave all valuables home when traveling abroad.

3) Yet, such arguments focus merely on theft, <u>without taking in account</u> other crimes.

4) <u>Believing</u> that the authorities turn a blind eye to such "soft" crimes, normally law-abiding tourists behave in this way because they <u>realize</u> that they can do so with impunity.

5) <u>Consider</u> the even more extreme case of tourists who go abroad to take advantage of that country's lack of enforcement of recreational drug use or prostitution.

6) Even though recreational drugs and prostitution are illegal in certain of these countries, some tourists again <u>believe</u> that they can justify their actions merely because of the fact that they will escape punishment.

7) Hence, these tourists fail to <u>consider</u> that these crimes are not enforced because of the country's economic conditions in the first place, and that by participating in these crimes, they are <u>exacerbating</u> and <u>perpetuating</u> crime even further in the host country.

ACT Essay Prompt 3

Now that you have completed the review exercises, you should attempt the following essay prompts as exam practice. Remember to allow 40 minutes to take each test. A model essay is provided in the next section.

Wherever we look in the world today, we can see advertisements for a variety of different products and brands. We see advertising on television and our devices, in addition to the traditional, outdoor forms of advertising. This proliferation of advertising introduces new products to the marketplace and provides us with information about items that may be of interest to us. Yet, might there be a dark side to this abundance of advertising? Because advertising has become so influential on us, the time has now come to analyze both the positive and negative effects it may be having upon us.

Perspective 1

Advertising is generally a waste of time and money. Most advertisements misrepresent or exaggerate products and beguile us with false information. For this reason, we would be well advised to ignore them.

Perspective 2

Advertising provides us with a great deal of important information. The impact of advertising means that the marketplace is more competitive, and this results in the best products reaching the consumer at the lowest prices.

Perspective 3

One should view advertisements with a critical mind. Because the companies backing their products are primarily driven by the impetus to improve their sales, we need to be discerning consumers.

Sample Essay 3

This essay is in response to the essay question from the practice test on the previous page. A detailed analysis of the essay is provided after the written essay response.

Advertising is a powerful force in today's materialistic, status-conscious society. Consumers are bombarded with advertising at every turn, from advertisements on television and radio, to outdoor advertising on electronic signs and even on buses. The abundance of advertising that confronts a person from one day to the next thus leaves one to wonder: How much of this advertising is really useful or necessary? This essay will reveal that while the majority of advertising serves only to drive mindless consumerism, a certain form of advertising does, in fact, serve a useful purpose.

Most advertising that we see nowadays, especially that on television, is the attempt of large companies to persuade the general public to buy products that they do not need, and may not ultimately want. In other words, advertisements do not truly exist to give product information to consumers, but rather to coerce them mentally into buying the product in question. Further, I would argue that this phenomenon has larger economic repercussions because it creates a false economy in which a demand is created for goods that are not really necessary. One only has to consider the amount of advertising for toys during children's TV programs to see this phenomenon in action. Perhaps the false economy created in this case is even more dreadful than it is normally, because it incites the demand for the product in question in children, who do not have the intellectual and developmental savvy to appreciate that they are being manipulated.

However, detractors to this viewpoint would claim that advertising nevertheless does provide information about products to consumers. They assert that, rather than producing a false economy, the practice of advertising helps to perpetuate competition and free enterprise in the marketplace and ultimately brings the best prices to customers. Under this view, advertising helps to sell goods to a larger market; therefore, as more goods are sold to the public, they become cheaper since they can be mass produced in order to meet demand.

But again, even a superficial analysis of this argument reveals that it is based on at least two obvious fallacies. First of all, sometimes the "information" provided in advertising is based on scant evidence, which is paraded as empirical proof in order to convince the consumer to buy. Take the advertising of cosmetics as a case in point. By now, many people will have seen the advertisement on television that states that 76% of the women tested felt that their wrinkles appeared to be visibly reduced after using a certain brand of face cream. Notice how carefully and manipulatively the advertisement is worded: "the women tested *felt* that their wrinkles *appeared* to be *visibly* reduced." The advertisement doesn't state that the condition of the women's skin actually improved from using the product. Notably, the "low price" argument also fails in this case as the women are encouraged to pay more for the product "because they're worth it."

Although I have enumerated what I see as the evils of advertising, I might be remiss if I did not concede that there is one case in which advertising does serve an extremely valuable purpose. I am speaking here about public service advertisements like those that warn against the dangers of driving while intoxicated or failing to wear a seat belt. Admittedly, these kinds of advertisements can literally have a very sobering effect.

So, what is the future of advertising? Should the government intervene to stamp down on the false or misleading claims that some advertisers attempt to make? It does in fact appear that a sea change may be beginning to take place already. For instance, some TV and magazine advertisements are now required to display footnotes at the bottom of the screen or page in order to qualify their claims. Providing information like this that clearly states the true limitations of products can only have a salutary effect. [646 words]

Analysis of Essay Structure in Sample Essay 3

First we will analyze the structure of the essay and the argumentative language the essay uses. On the following pages, we will analyze the writer's use of linking words, adjectives, modality, qualifiers, and verbs.

This essay uses a "scheme 1" organizational scheme.

Assertion – The primary assertion is in the last sentence of paragraph 1: "while the majority of advertising serves only to drive mindless consumerism, a certain form of advertising does, in fact, serve a useful purpose."

The argumentative language from this paragraph is: "the abundance of" and "How much of . . . is really useful or necessary?"

Argument 1 – The writer's first argument is in paragraph 2. It is that advertising "persuade[s] the general public to buy products that they do not need" and thereby creates a "false economy."

The argumentative language from this paragraph is: "I would argue that" and "One only has to consider."

Counterargument 1 – Counterargument 1 is in paragraph 3. It is that advertising is necessary because it "provide[s] information about products to consumers" and "brings the best prices" to them.

The argumentative language from this paragraph is: "detractors to this viewpoint would claim that," "They assert that" and "under this view."

Argument 2 – Argument 2 is in paragraph 4. It is that sometimes the information provided in advertising is misleading and that sometimes companies actually increase the price of their product.

The argumentative language from this paragraph is: an "analysis of this argument reveals that it is based on . . . fallacies" and "Take . . . as a case in point."

In the fifth paragraph, the writer makes an exception for public service advertising.

Synthesis – The synthesis of the essay is found in the two rhetorical questions: "So, what is the future of advertising?" and "Should the government intervene to stamp down on the false or misleading claims that some advertisers attempt to make?"

Conclusion – The writer's conclusion is: "Providing information like this that clearly states the true limitations of products can only have a salutary effect."

Analysis of Linking Words and Verbs in Sample Essay 3

As stated in the units at the beginning of this publication, you can use linking words, adjectives, modality, qualifiers, and verbs to make your ACT essay more effective. Pay particular attention to the highlighted **linking words**, *adjectives,* and <u>verbs</u> in sample essay 3 below.

Advertising is a *powerful* force in today's materialistic, status-conscious society. Consumers are bombarded with advertising at every turn, from advertisements on television and radio, to outdoor advertising on electronic signs and even on buses. The abundance of advertising that confronts a person from one day to the next **thus** leaves one to wonder: How much of this advertising is really *useful* or *necessary*? This essay will <u>reveal</u> that **while** the majority of advertising serves only to drive *mindless* consumerism, a certain form of advertising does, **in fact**, serve a useful purpose.

Most advertising that we see nowadays, especially that on television, is the attempt of large companies to <u>persuade</u> the general public to buy products that they do not need, and may not ultimately want. **In other words**, advertisements do not truly exist to give product information to consumers, **but rather** to <u>coerce</u> them mentally into buying the product in question. **Further**, I would argue that this phenomenon has larger economic repercussions **because** it creates a false economy in which a demand is created for goods that are not really necessary. One only has to consider the amount of advertising for toys during children's TV programs to see this phenomenon in action. Perhaps the false economy created in this case is even more *dreadful* than it is normally, **because** it incites the demand for the product in question in children, who do not have the intellectual and developmental savvy to appreciate that they are being manipulated.

However, detractors to this viewpoint would claim that advertising **nevertheless** does provide information about products to consumers. They assert that, **rather than** producing a false economy, the practice of advertising helps to perpetuate competition and free enterprise in the marketplace and ultimately brings the best prices to customers. **Under this view,** advertising helps to sell goods to a larger market; **therefore**, as more goods are sold to the public, they become cheaper **since** they can be mass produced in order to meet demand.

Yet again, even a superficial analysis of this argument reveals that it is based on at least two *obvious* fallacies. **First of all**, sometimes the "information" provided in advertising is based on *scant* evidence, which is paraded as empirical proof in order to convince the consumer to buy. Take the advertising of cosmetics as a case in point. By now, many people will have seen the advertisement on television that states that 76% of the women tested felt that their wrinkles appeared to be visibly reduced after using a certain brand of face cream. Notice how carefully and manipulatively the advertisement is worded: "the women tested felt that their wrinkles appeared to be visibly reduced." The advertisement doesn't state that the condition of the women's skin actually improved from using the product. Notably, the "low price" argument **also** fails in this case **as** the women are encouraged to pay more for the product "because they're worth it."

Although I have enumerated what I see as the evils of advertising, I might be remiss if I did not concede that there is one case in which advertising does serve an extremely *valuable* purpose. I am speaking here about public service advertisements like those that warn against the dangers of driving while intoxicated or failing to wear a seat belt. Admittedly, these kinds of advertisements can literally have a very sobering effect.

So, what is the future of advertising? Should the government intervene to stamp down on the false or misleading claims that some advertisers attempt to make? It does **in fact** appear that a sea change may be beginning to take place already. **For instance**, some TV and magazine advertisements are now required to display footnotes at the bottom of the screen or page in order to qualify their claims. Providing information like this that clearly states the true limitations of products can only have a *salutary* effect.

Analysis of Modality and Qualifiers in Sample Essay 3

Now look at essay 3 again, noting the use of <u>modality</u> and **qualifiers**.

Advertising is a powerful force in today's materialistic, status-conscious society. Consumers are bombarded with advertising at every turn, from advertisements on television and radio, to outdoor advertising on electronic signs and even on buses. The abundance of advertising that confronts a person from one day to the next thus leaves one to wonder: How much of this advertising is really useful or necessary? This essay will reveal that while the majority of advertising serves only to drive mindless consumerism, a certain form of advertising does, in fact, serve a useful purpose.

Most advertising that we see nowadays, especially that on television, is the attempt of large companies to persuade the general public to buy products that they do not need, and <u>may</u> not ultimately want. In other words, advertisements do not truly exist to give product information to consumers, but rather to coerce them mentally into buying the product in question. Further, I <u>would</u> argue that this phenomenon has larger economic repercussions because it creates a false economy in which a demand is created for goods that are not really necessary. One only has to consider the amount of advertising for toys during children's TV programs to see this phenomenon in action. Perhaps the false economy created in this case is even more dreadful than it is normally, because it incites the demand for the product in question in children, who do not have the intellectual and developmental savvy to appreciate that they are being manipulated.

However, detractors to this viewpoint <u>would</u> claim that advertising nevertheless does provide information about products to consumers. They assert that, rather than producing a false economy, the practice of advertising helps to perpetuate competition and free enterprise in the marketplace and ultimately brings the best prices to customers. Under this view, advertising helps to sell goods to a larger market; therefore, as more goods are sold to the public, they become cheaper since they can be mass produced in order to meet demand.

Yet again, even a superficial analysis of this argument reveals that it is based on at least two obvious fallacies. First of all, sometimes the "information" provided in advertising is based on scant evidence, which is paraded as empirical proof in order to convince the consumer to buy. Take the advertising of cosmetics as a case in point. By now, many people will have seen the advertisement on television that states that 76% of the women tested felt that their wrinkles appeared to be visibly reduced after using a certain brand of face cream. Notice how carefully and manipulatively the advertisement is worded: "the women tested felt that their wrinkles appeared to be visibly reduced." The advertisement doesn't state that the condition of the women's skin actually improved from using the product. **Notably**, the "low price" argument also fails in this case as the women are encouraged to pay more for the product "because they're worth it."

Although I have enumerated what I see as the evils of advertising, I <u>might</u> be remiss if I did not concede that there is one case in which advertising does serve an extremely valuable purpose. I am speaking here about public service advertisements like those that warn against the dangers of driving while intoxicated or failing to wear a seat belt. **Admittedly**, these kinds of advertisements <u>can</u> literally have a very sobering effect.

So, what is the future of advertising? <u>Should</u> the government intervene to stamp down on the false or misleading claims that some advertisers attempt to make? It does in fact appear that a sea change <u>may</u> be beginning to take place already. For instance, some

TV and magazine advertisements are now required to display footnotes at the bottom of the screen or page in order to qualify their claims. Providing information like this that clearly states the true limitations of products <u>can</u> only have a salutary effect.

ACT Essay Prompt 4

You are allowed 40 minutes to take this test. A model essay is provided in the next section.

The internet is certainly a useful source of information, in addition to offering services online. From ordering a meal to checking a bank account, we are now able to perform tasks at home that we previously would have had to do in person. Sharing personal news is also easier than ever before thanks to the plethora of available social media platforms. However, is all of this information accessibility and sharing an undisputably good thing? With the prevalence of the internet in our daily lives, it is now worth examining this issue in a discerning manner.

Perspective 1

The internet provides far too much unreliable information, not to mention material that is objectionable or offensive for other reasons. The government should act now in order to regulate the online industry.

Perspective 2

Without the availability of the internet, we would easily have to spend two additional hours every day to do things like shopping and communicating with friends. Since the internet is so essential, users should be able to access it freely, without regulation.

Perspective 3

The internet may be useful for things like shopping or socializing, but one needs to be more careful when accessing information. This is especially true for sites relating to finances or personal health.

Sample Essay 4

This essay is in response to the essay question on the previous page. A detailed analysis of the essay is provided after the written essay response.

In today's digital and electronic age, it almost goes without question that the internet is practical for our daily lives because it makes some mundane tasks more convenient. For instance, gone are the days when one had to go to the travel agent and sit in front of a desk while the agent looked through offers on his or her screen. Internet users can now book airline tickets and make travel arrangements in the comfort of their own living rooms with the click of a mouse. But in spite of the numerous conveniences of the internet, there are those who hold the view that the internet contains a great deal of worthless, harmful, and offensive information and that the internet can be used to perpetrate deception and even crime. It appears that although the internet can be a useful tool in many ways, it needs to be used cautiously, and should even be regulated, in some circumstances.

It is an undeniable facet of modern life that the internet is useful for our communication needs and for making social contacts. Remember the days when one had to post a letter to communicate with someone overseas? Those days are in the past now thanks to the wonder of email, direct messaging, online chat, and social networking sites. Still, others would maintain that often these social contacts are the breeding ground for dishonest or even criminally-minded individuals who want to prey on the weak and vulnerable. We have heard numerous stories of adolescents who are lured away from home to meet someone that they have communicated with online. Regrettably, in the end, the person making contact turns out to be a sexual predator intent on harming the young person. Such an experience, certainly, would negatively influence the child during the formative years of his or her personality development.

In addition to the double-edged sword effect of the communications capabilities of the internet, there is no disputing that the internet gives us ready access to a great deal of information. Indeed, some websites contain indispensable factual information for daily life and health. Consider the case of someone who wants to quit smoking. He or she can go to websites like the one run by the American Cancer Society to get the help and support needed to give up. Many of these types of websites are established by governmental agencies or charitable organizations, so the user can be confident that the information contained on these sites is trustworthy. On the other hand, however, one must also concede that much of the so-called "information" on the internet needs to be read with a critical mind. Since anyone can set up a website, the qualifications of the site owner, as well as the accuracy and quality of the information on the site need to be perused skeptically. The rise of medical forums run by people with no medical training whatsoever and the abundance of online shops selling discount medications are a particular worry, as some people will rely on these websites to make a self-diagnosis and then purchase medicine, without taking heed of the possibility that the medicine could potentially kill them.

Yet, others would suggest that the media has seriously exaggerated the number of incidents of internet users being grievously harmed or killed by people they have met or products they have purchased on the internet and that the very large majority of the population have the common sense to know what is dangerous or not. But what about the minority of people who do not? Will they remain unprotected just to accommodate the desires of the majority? It is true that internet usage needs to be approached vigilantly on certain occasions. The internet may need to face governmental regulation in the future, but that regulation will need to be moderate, because if the internet becomes too highly regulated, it will lose a great deal of the convenience that it already affords us.

[657 words]

Analysis of Essay Structure in Sample Essay 4

As before, we will analyze the structure of the essay and the argumentative language the essay uses. On the following pages, we will analyze the writer's use of linking words, adjectives, modality, qualifiers, and verbs.

This essay uses a "scheme 2" organizational scheme.

Assertion – The primary assertion is in the last sentence of paragraph 1: "although . . . the internet can be a useful tool in many ways, it needs to be used cautiously, and should even be regulated, in some circumstances."

The argumentative language from this paragraph is: "it almost goes without question that" and "there are those who hold the view that."

Argument 1 – The writer's first argument in paragraph 2. It is that "the internet is useful for our communication needs and for making social contacts."

Counterargument 1 – Counterargument 1 is in the second part of paragraph 2. It is that "these social contacts are the breeding ground for dishonest or even criminally-minded individuals who want to prey on the weak and vulnerable."

The argumentative language from this paragraph is: "others would maintain that" and "We have heard numerous stories of."

Argument 2 – Argument 2 is in paragraph 3. It is that "the internet gives us ready access to a great deal of information."

Counterargument 2 – Counterargument 2 is in the second half of paragraph 3. It is that "much of the so-called "information" on the internet needs to be read with a critical mind."

The argumentative language from this paragraph is: "the double-edged sword effect of," "there is no disputing that," "Consider the case of," "one must also concede that" and " . . . are a particular worry."

Synthesis – The synthesis of the essay is found in the first half of the last paragraph. It is "But what about the minority of people who do not [know what is dangerous]? Will they remain unprotected just to accommodate the desires of the majority?"

Conclusion – The writer's conclusion is: "The internet may need to face governmental regulation in the future, but that regulation will need to be moderate, because if the internet becomes too highly regulated, it will lose a great deal of the convenience that it already affords us."

Analysis of Linking Words and Verbs in Sample Essay 4

Pay particular attention to the highlighted **linking words**, *adjectives,* and <u>verbs</u> in sample essay 4 below.

In today's digital and electronic age, it almost goes without question that the internet is *practical* for our daily lives because it makes some mundane tasks more convenient. **For instance**, gone are the days when one had to go to the travel agent and sit in front of a desk while the agent looked through offers on his or her screen. Internet users can now book airline tickets and make travel arrangements in the comfort of their own living rooms with the click of a mouse. **But in spite of** the numerous conveniences of the internet, there are those who <u>hold</u> the view that the internet contains a great deal of *worthless*, *harmful,* and *offensive* information and that the internet can be used to <u>perpetrate</u> deception and even crime. It appears that **although** the internet can be a *useful* tool in many ways, it needs to be used cautiously, and should even be regulated, in some circumstances.

It is an *undeniable* facet of modern life that the internet is useful for our communication needs and for making social contacts. Remember the days when one had to post a letter to communicate with someone overseas? Those days are in the past now thanks to the wonder of email, direct messaging, online chat, and social networking sites. **Still**, others would <u>maintain</u> that often these social contacts are the breeding ground for *dishonest* or even *criminally-minded* individuals who want to prey on the weak and vulnerable. We have heard numerous stories of adolescents who are lured away from home to meet someone that they have communicated with online. Regrettably, in the end, the person making contact turns out to be a sexual predator intent on harming the young person.

Such an experience, certainly, would negatively influence the child during the formative years of his or her personality development.

In addition to the double-edged sword effect of the communications capabilities of the internet, there is no disputing that the internet gives us ready access to a great deal of information. **Indeed**, some websites contain *indispensable* factual information for daily life and health. Consider the case of someone who wants to quit smoking. He or she can go to websites like the one run by the American Cancer Society to get the help and support needed to give up. Many of these types of websites are established by governmental agencies or charitable organizations, **so** the user can be confident that the information contained on these sites is *trustworthy*. **On the other hand, however**, one must also concede that much of the so-called "information" on the internet needs to be read with a *critical* mind. **Since** anyone can set up a website, the qualifications of the site owner, **as well as** the accuracy and quality of the information on the site need to be perused skeptically. The rise of medical forums run by people with no medical training whatsoever and the abundance of online shops selling discount medications are a particular worry, **as** some people will rely on these websites to make a self-diagnosis and then purchase medicine, without taking heed of the possibility that the medicine could potentially kill them.

Yet, others would suggest that the media has seriously exaggerated the number of incidents of internet users being grievously harmed or killed by people they have met or products they have purchased on the internet and that the very large majority of the population have the common sense to know what is dangerous or not. But what about the minority of people who do not? Will they remain unprotected just to accommodate the desires of the majority? It is true that internet usage needs to be approached vigilantly on certain occasions. The internet may need to face governmental regulation in the future, but that regulation would need to be *moderate*, **because** if the internet becomes too highly regulated, it will lose a great deal of the convenience that it already affords us.

Analysis of Modality and Qualifiers in Sample Essay 4

Now look at essay 4 again, noting the use of <u>modality</u> and **qualifiers**.

In today's digital and electronic age, it almost goes without question that the internet is practical for our daily lives because it makes some mundane tasks more convenient. For instance, gone are the days when one had to go to the travel agent and sit in front of a desk while the agent looked through offers on his or her screen. Internet users can now book airline tickets and make travel arrangements in the comfort of their own living rooms with the click of a mouse. But in spite of the numerous conveniences of the internet, there are those who hold the view that the internet contains a great deal of worthless, harmful, and offensive information and that the internet <u>can</u> be used to perpetrate deception and even crime. It appears that although the internet <u>can</u> be a useful tool in many ways, it needs to be used cautiously, and <u>should</u> even be regulated, in some circumstances.

It is an undeniable facet of modern life that the internet is useful for our communication needs and for making social contacts. Remember the days when one had to post a letter to communicate with someone overseas? Those days are in the past now thanks to the wonder of email, direct messaging, online chat, and social networking sites. Still, others <u>would</u> maintain that often these social contacts are the breeding ground for dishonest or even criminally-minded individuals who want to prey on the weak and vulnerable. We have heard numerous stories of adolescents who are lured away from home to meet someone that they have communicated with online. **Regrettably**, in the end, the person making contact turns out to be a sexual predator intent on harming the young person. Such an experience, **certainly**, would negatively influence the child during the formative years of his or her personality development.

In addition to the double-edged sword effect of the communications capabilities of the internet, there is no disputing that the internet gives us ready access to a great deal of information. Indeed, some websites contain indispensable factual information for daily life and health. Consider the case of someone who wants to quit smoking. He or she can go to websites like the one run by the American Cancer Society to get the help and support needed to give up. Many of these types of websites are established by governmental agencies or charitable organizations, so the user can be confident that the information contained on these sites is trustworthy. On the other hand, however, one must also concede that much of the so-called "information" on the internet needs to be read with a critical mind. Since anyone can set up a website, the qualifications of the site owner, as well as the accuracy and quality of the information on the site need to be perused skeptically. The rise of medical forums run by people with no medical training whatsoever and the abundance of online shops selling discount medications are a particular worry, as some people will rely on these websites to make a self-diagnosis and then purchase medicine, without taking heed of the possibility that the medicine could potentially kill them.

Yet, others would suggest that the media has seriously exaggerated the number of incidents of internet users being grievously harmed or killed by people they have met or products they have purchased on the internet and that the very large majority of the population have the common sense to know what is dangerous or not. But what about the minority of people who do not? Will they remain unprotected just to accommodate the desires of the majority? It is true that internet usage needs to be approached vigilantly on certain occasions. The internet may need to face governmental regulation in the future, but that regulation will need to be moderate, because if the internet becomes too highly regulated, it will lose a great deal of the convenience that it already affords us.

ACT Essay Prompt 5

Allow 40 minutes to take this test. A model response is provided in the next section.

Certain cases about the "right to die" have been well-publicized in the press. Families have recounted their stories of personal sadness about seeing a loved one suffer while on life support. Yet, other families have spoken out with anger about having to terminate life support because the hospital has mandated it. Should euthanasia be considered to be a basic human right? Since the wishes of the family and the patient may be at odds, this issue needs to be examined in detail.

Perspective 1

The suffering that terminally-ill individuals experience can severely limit their quality of life. Those with terminal, incurable illnesses should be allowed to choose to die, especially if they are in intense pain.

Perspective 2

Legalizing euthanasia would be a huge mistake in some situations. This is especially true if the patient is no longer conscious, since those making the decision to end the patient's life could have selfish motives.

Perspective 3

Deciding to end someone else's life, even that of someone who has a terminal condition, is always morally wrong. Miracle recoveries happen every day and people should not be allowed to play God.

Sample Essay 5

This essay is in response to the essay question on the previous page. A detailed analysis of the essay is provided after the written essay response.

Modern advancements in science and medicine have meant that life expectancy is much longer now than in the past. A number of previously fatal conditions and illness, such as having the HIV virus, can now be addressed with the use of medications and other treatments because of modern science. Yet, in some cases, the life that the seriously ill person lives is full of pain and suffering. Would it be more humane in these cases to permit euthanasia? The choice about receiving medical treatment or not during life-threatening conditions is one that ought to be very strictly controlled and is one that can be answered competently only if we first respond to two other questions: Who should decide what the best course of action is in each individual case and under what conditions?

Clearly, pain and suffering are very individual and private experiences as each person has a very different threshold for and tolerance of pain. Patients who have been diagnosed with terminal, incurable illnesses and have been given months to live might prefer not to live during those remaining months if there is going to be a great deal of intense suffering. In essence, the question revolves around the quality of the patient's remaining life. Nevertheless, opponents to this viewpoint are quick to point out that misdiagnoses are made and that patients do sometimes make unexplained recoveries after having received grim prognoses. But experience tells us that this is normally not the case: miraculous recoveries are few and far between in reality, and having false hope generally only works to prolong suffering and a poor quality of life.

The "quality of life" argument is particularly persuasive when the patient shows no brain activity and is being kept alive on a life support machine. If our loved one is mentally incapacitated, he or she cannot make a decision about his or her own welfare. Who then should? Is it right for family members to decide? The problem is that family members, already struggling to come to terms with their loved one's grave condition, are now placed in the unenviable position of having to make an agonizing choice. They may ask themselves what their loved one would have wanted, but in the end, such decisions are made under great mental duress and may be decisions that the family members ultimately live to regret.

However, the argument above is based on the presumption that the family relationship is amicable and that family members will always place a priority on the wishes of their loved one. What happens when this is not the case? In the most extreme case, this argument holds that family members might act to hasten the death of the patient in order to put an end to an acrimonious family life, to be able to collect inheritance and insurance pay-outs, or both. Avarice, they claim, is a more powerful human motivator than love, so consider the power of greed when love has ceased to exist. Surely, they assert, we should not let those who stand to gain from the patient's death make the very decision that the patient should die.

In order to attempt to address the murky issues surrounding euthanasia, several countries are now recognizing Advance Health Directives as a matter of law. The directive, which the individual must make when he or she is of sound mind, stipulates the conditions for the receipt of medical treatment and hospital care. The legal document must be signed and sworn and is valid only when and if the person giving the directive is unable to provide consent because of mental incapacity. Such a document effectively removes the need for family members to ponder the wishes of the patient since the patient has already committed his or her wishes to writing. The document also protects the patient in the event that unscrupulous family members may want to hasten the patient's death for personal or financial reasons. While the debate about euthanasia *per se* might continue in cases where the patient has not expressed his or her wishes beforehand, Advance Health Directives are certainly a positive step in addressing the issue. [689 words]

Analysis of Essay Structure in Sample Essay 5

The structure of the essay and the argumentative language the essay uses are analyzed below. On the following pages, the writer's use of linking words, adjectives, modality, qualifiers, and verbs is analyzed.

This essay uses a "scheme 2" organizational scheme.

Assertion – The primary assertion is in the last sentence of paragraph 1: "The choice about receiving medical treatment or not during life-threatening conditions is one that ought to be very strictly controlled and is one that can be answered competently only if we first respond to two other questions: Who should decide what the best course of action is in each individual case and under what conditions?"

The argumentative language from this paragraph is: "have meant that" and "in some cases."

Argument 1 – The writer's first argument in paragraph 2. It is that "Patients who have been diagnosed with terminal, incurable illnesses and have been given months to live might prefer not to live during those remaining months if there is going to be a great deal of intense suffering."

Counterargument 1 – Counterargument 1 is in the second half of paragraph 2. It is that "misdiagnoses are made and that patients do sometimes make unexplained recoveries after having received grim prognoses."

The argumentative language from this paragraph is: "the question revolves around," "opponents to this viewpoint," "experience tells us that," "so-called," and "in reality."

Argument 2 – Argument 2 is in paragraph 3. It is that the "quality of life argument is particularly persuasive when the patient shows no brain activity and is being kept alive on a life support machine."

The argumentative language from this paragraph is: "argument is particularly persuasive when," "Is it right for . . . to," "The problem is that" and "They may ask themselves."

Counterargument 2 – Counterargument 2 is in paragraph 4. It is that there are flaws in the argument that "the family relationship is amicable and that family members will always place a priority on the wishes of their loved one."

The argumentative language from this paragraph is: "the argument above is based on the presumption that . . . ," "What happens when this is not the case?," "In the most extreme case," "this argument holds that . . . ," "they claim," "so consider," and "they assert."

Synthesis – The synthesis of the essay is found in the last paragraph. It is that "In order to attempt to address the murky issues surrounding euthanasia, several countries are now recognizing Advance Health Directives as a matter of law."

Conclusion – The writer's conclusion is: "While the debate about euthanasia *per se* might continue in cases where the patient has not expressed his or her wishes beforehand, Advance Health Directives are certainly a positive step in addressing the issue."

Analysis of Linking Words and Verbs in Sample Essay 5

Pay particular attention to the highlighted **linking words**, *adjectives,* and <u>verbs</u> in sample essay 5 below.

Modern advancements in science and medicine have meant that life expectancy is much longer now than in the past. A number of previously fatal conditions and illness, such as having the HIV virus, can now be addressed with the use of medications and other treatments because of modern science. **Yet**, in some cases, the life that the seriously ill person lives is full of pain and suffering. Would it be more humane in these cases to permit euthanasia? The choice about receiving medical treatment or not during life-threatening conditions is one that ought to be very strictly controlled and is one that can be answered competently only if we **first** respond to two other questions: Who should decide what the *best* course of action is in each individual case and under what conditions?

Clearly, pain and suffering are very *individual* and *private* experiences as each person has a very *different* threshold for and tolerance of pain. Patients who have been diagnosed with terminal, incurable illnesses and have been given months to live might prefer not to live during those remaining months if there is going to be a great deal of *intense* suffering. **In essence**, the question revolves around the quality of the patient's remaining life. **Nevertheless**, opponents to this viewpoint are quick to <u>point out</u> that misdiagnoses are made and that patients do sometimes make unexplained recoveries after having received *grim* prognoses. But experience tells us that this is normally not the case: miraculous recoveries are few and far between in reality, and having false hope generally only works to prolong suffering and a *poor* quality of life.

The "quality of life" argument is particularly *persuasive* **when** the patient shows no brain activity and is being kept alive on a life support machine. If our loved one is mentally incapacitated, he or she cannot make a decision about his or her own welfare. Who then should? Is it right for family members to decide? The problem is that family members, already struggling to come to terms with their loved one's *grave* condition, are now placed in the *unenviable* position of having to make an *agonizing* choice. They may ask themselves what their loved one would have wanted, but in the end, such decisions are made under great mental duress and may be decisions that the family members ultimately live to regret.

However, the argument above is based on the presumption that the family relationship is *amicable* and that family members will always place a priority on the wishes of their loved one. What happens when this is not the case? In the most extreme case, this argument holds that family members might act to hasten the death of the patient in order to put an end to an *acrimonious* family life, to be able to collect inheritance and insurance pay-outs, or both. Avarice, they claim, is a more powerful human motivator than love, **so** consider the power of greed when love has ceased to exist. Surely, they assert, we should not let those who stand to gain from the patient's death make the very decision that the patient should die.

In order to attempt to address the *murky* issues surrounding euthanasia, several countries are now recognizing Advance Health Directives as a matter of law. The directive, which the individual must make when he or she is of sound mind, stipulates the conditions for the receipt of medical treatment and hospital care. The legal document must be signed and sworn and is valid only when and if the person giving the directive is unable to provide consent **because of** mental incapacity. Such a document effectively removes the need for family members to ponder the wishes of the patient **since** the patient has already committed his or her wishes to writing. The document **also** protects the patient in the event that *unscrupulous* family members may want to hasten the patient's death for personal or financial reasons. **While** the debate about euthanasia per se might continue in cases where the patient has not expressed his or her wishes beforehand, Advance Health Directives are certainly a *positive* step in addressing the issue.

Analysis of Modality and Qualifiers in Sample Essay 5

Now look at essay 5 again, noting the use of <u>modality</u> and **qualifiers**.

Modern advancements in science and medicine have meant that life expectancy is much longer now than in the past. A number of previously fatal conditions and illness, such as having the HIV virus, can now be addressed with the use of medications and other treatments because of modern science. Yet, in some cases, the life that the seriously ill person lives is full of pain and suffering. <u>Would</u> it be more humane in these cases to permit euthanasia? The choice about receiving medical treatment or not during life-threatening conditions is one that <u>ought</u> to be very strictly controlled and is one that can be answered competently only if we first respond to two other questions: Who <u>should</u> decide what the best course of action is in each individual case and under what conditions?

Clearly, pain and suffering are very individual and private experiences as each person has a very different threshold for and tolerance of pain. Patients who have been diagnosed with terminal, incurable illnesses and have been given months to live <u>might</u> prefer not to live during those remaining months if there is going to be a great deal of intense suffering. In essence, the question revolves around the quality of the patient's remaining life. Nevertheless, opponents to this viewpoint are quick to point out that misdiagnoses are made and that patients do sometimes make unexplained recoveries after having received grim prognoses. But experience tells us that this is normally not the case: miraculous recoveries are few and far between in reality, and having false hope generally only works to prolong suffering and a poor quality of life.

The "quality of life" argument is **particularly** persuasive when the patient shows no brain activity and is being kept alive on a life support machine. If our loved one is mentally incapacitated, he or she cannot make a decision about his or her own welfare. Who then should? Is it right for family members to decide? The problem is that family members, already struggling to come to terms with their loved one's grave condition, are now placed in the unenviable position of having to make an agonizing choice. They may ask themselves what their loved one would have wanted, but in the end, such decisions are made under great mental duress and may be decisions that the family members ultimately live to regret.

However, the argument above is based on the presumption that the family relationship is amicable and that family members will always place a priority on the wishes of their loved one. What happens when this is not the case? In the most extreme case, this argument holds that family members might act to hasten the death of the patient in order to put an end to an acrimonious family life, to be able to collect inheritance and insurance pay-outs, or both. Avarice, they claim, is a more powerful human motivator than love, so consider the power of greed when love has ceased to exist. Surely, they assert, we should not let those who stand to gain from the patient's death make the very decision that the patient should die.

In order to attempt to address the murky issues surrounding euthanasia, several countries are now recognizing Advance Health Directives as a matter of law. The directive, which the individual must make when he or she is of sound mind, stipulates the conditions for the receipt of medical treatment and hospital care. The legal document must be signed and sworn and is valid only when and if the person giving the directive is unable to provide consent because of mental incapacity. Such a document effectively removes the need for family members to ponder the wishes of the patient since the patient has already committed his or her wishes to writing. The document also protects the patient in the event that unscrupulous family members may want to hasten the patient's death for personal or financial reasons. While the debate about euthanasia per se might continue in cases where the patient has not expressed his or her wishes beforehand, Advance Health Directives are **certainly** a positive step in addressing the issue.

Additional ACT Essay Prompts

In this part of the study guide, we are providing additional essay prompts to help you practice your essay writing skills for the ACT.

Allow yourself 40 minutes to complete each one, using the tips and suggestions from this study guide.

ACT Essay Prompt 6

Scientific research using animals as subjects is a controversial practice. These experiments are carried out on animals such as laboratory mice or rats since doing so on humans would be considered cruel or immoral. However, animals may be made to suffer when undergoing tests for new medical procedures, pharmaceutical drugs, or even cosmetics. This begs the question: It is right to use animals for research purposes in this way? Since this topic has become so contentious recently, the practice should certainly be evaluated.

Perspective 1

All animal testing for scientific reasons should be banned now and always. The life of an animal is just as precious as that of a human being, so it is unethical to use animals in this way.

Perspective 2

According to the concept of evolution, some species can be considered more developed than others. Human beings have evolved to be dominant over other creatures, so we should have no qualms about using animals for research purposes.

Perspective 3

Conducting research on animal subjects should be permitted only in certain situations. While it may be acceptable to use animals for medical research, the practice should be banned for frivolous purposes, such as testing cosmetics.

ACT Essay Prompt 7

Many students dream of attending prestigious universities such as Harvard or Oxford. Residential academies, also called boarding schools, can be a positive step on the career path of students with aspirations such as these. However, children usually suffer from homesickness and a degree of separation anxiety when adjusting to life away from home. Is it ever a good idea to send a child away to residential academies like this? Because of the potential phycological damage to the children involved, this topic is worthy of debate.

Perspective 1

Parents should not be allowed to send children to boarding school without the child's consent. Residential academies are often used by lazy parents who just want to be spared the hard work of raising a child.

Perspective 2

Children should be sent to boarding schools whenever the parents can afford to do so. Living away from home helps to build character and confidence, as well as improving academic and social skills.

Perspective 3

Parents should think carefully before sending children away from home to study. If an academically gifted student has to drive to study away from home, then parents should talk to their child about it and try to make this dream a reality.

ACT Essay Prompt 8

Many people believe in the expression: "An eye for an eye; a tooth for a tooth." Because of this notion, they assert that murderers should be put to death for the crimes they commit. Yet, others are opposed to the death penalty since they claim that taking any life is always immoral. Should the death penalty be reinstated nationwide for all those convicted of murder? This issue is extremely urgent, especially for those currently on death row, so the topic requires dispassionate analysis.

Perspective 1

The death penalty serves as a deterrent for capital murder and often effectively dissuades people who would otherwise lash out against others. When people take a life, they should know that they will also lose their lives.

Perspective 2

The death penalty should be reserved only for especially heinous crimes, such as serial murders or the killing of young children. Killing offenders without providing them a second chance is not how we should behave in a civilized society.

Perspective 3

Taking a life is never acceptable, whether a person has committed a wrong or not. Putting a murderer to death does not bring back the deceased, and offenders should be given the opportunity to reform.

ACT Essay Prompt 9

According to an old expression: "No one knows what goes on behind closed doors." Couples who appear to have harmonious relationships when out in public may be suffering from abuse from a partner at home. Indeed, statistics reveal that both men and women now suffer from domestic violence. Should the government or police do more to address the issue of domestic abuse? As serious domestic assault can end in the death on one or both partners, we must now examine this problem.

Perspective 1

More serious penalties should be put in place for repeat offenders of domestic abuse. In addition, it should not be possible for victims to retract their complaints of abuse once they return home, since such retractions are usually made at the perpetrator's behest.

Perspective 2

The responsibility for domestic violence rests primarily with the individual. What is needed is more education and help for victims attempting to leave home, rather than intervention by law.

Perspective 3

Domestic violence should always be classified as a criminal offense, regardless of the extent of injury inflicted upon the victim. The police need to jail offenders quickly, and new laws need to be put in place to make punishments more severe.

ACT Essay Prompt 10

Whether to be used for recreation of for pain relief, marijuana can be purchased in stores legally in some states in the US. Some believe that marijuana should be fully legalized in all states, while others have serious reservations about this idea. However, do the advantages of legalizing marijuana outweigh the disadvantages? Since marijuana usage has increased and laws are constantly being relaxed, it is necessary to reassess this situation.

Perspective 1

All marijuana usage should be made illegal. It is well known that marijuana is often used as a gateway to more serious drugs, such as cocaine and heroin, and drug abuse is at an all-time high in our nation.

Perspective 2

If we truly live in a democratic country, people should be free to do what they want to do. Marijuana use should be made legal nationwide to increase personal freedom and to reduce the amount of public money wasted on trying to enforce antiquated laws.

Perspective 3

Marijuana should be made legal, but only for medical use. Cannabis products are helpful for a number of medical conditions, and medical usage could be easily granted through a prescription from a physician.

ACT Essay Prompt 11

Social media platforms help us connect with friends and feel closer to the ones we love. However, these platforms can also be used by "trolls" who use hateful or inflammatory comments that greatly distress others. For this reason, should censorship in social media should be considered a necessary evil? There have been several notable cases in which victims have committed suicide as a result of online abuse, so we must now address this exigent issue.

Perspective 1

Social media platforms have become a breeding ground for a new generation of online bullies. Social media providers need to do much more to regulate the content that users post on their platforms.

Perspective 2

Trolls are simply cowards since they say things online that they would never say face-to-face. On the other hand, the use of social media is not compulsory, so those who feel offended should simply delete their accounts.

Perspective 3

Users of social media are often far too sensitive and need to be much more thick-skinned. The control of social media would place serious restrictions on how these platforms are used and greatly limit our interactions with others.

ACT Essay Prompt 12

In today's image-conscious society, people are becoming more aware of their appearance than ever before. Some people think that a cosmetic procedure would help to boost their self-esteem and make them feel better. It is no surprise then that cosmetic surgery has become big business. What is your response to the view that the government should intervene to regulate cosmetic surgery? Due to the fact that some cosmetic surgeons are not licensed to conduct the operations that they perform on their patients, this problem requires careful consideration.

Perspective 1

No one is ever forced to undergo a cosmetic procedure since such operations are, by their nature, not medically necessary. Those who wish to improve their looks in this way should simply accept the existing risks involved.

Perspective 2

Cosmetic procedures are never risk-free undertakings since they involve being placed under anesthetic and having surgery performed on some part of the body. The government should therefore control cosmetic procedures in the same way that surgeons are regulated.

Perspective 3

Cosmetic surgery should be regulated, but not as vigorously as other surgeries. If too many controls are put in place on cosmetic procedures, the provider's insurance will skyrocket, making such procedures unaffordable for a great many people who desire them.

ACT Essay Prompt 13

The generation gap seems to have existed for time immemorial, and older people sometimes lament what they see as the lack of value that the younger generation places on hard work. However, younger people sometimes already feel exhausted from the effort they put in at the workplace, not to mention the effort required at home. How should we respond to the statement: "Young people nowadays should be required to do a stint of manual labor to show them what a hard day's work is"? Since hard physical work can strengthen the body and mind, this topic is deserving of discussion.

Perspective 1

Young people have to work harder now than past generations ever did. Younger workers not only have to keep pace with relentless technological changes in the workplace, but also have to look for and keep work in a much more competitive job market.

Perspective 2

Innovation and technology have made the younger generation lazy both mentally and physically. A day of work in a factory or on a farm would build their characters and make them more appreciative of their lives.

Perspective 3

Hard physical labor should only be reserved for young people who want to do so or for those who cannot get any other types of work. In addition, manual labor could be used to help people overcome crime or addiction.

ACT Essay Prompt 14

Laws are in place to make smoking illegal in certain states in many public places, such as in theaters or restaurants. Nevertheless, smokers may resent the limitations placed on their desire to smoke where there wish, especially in places where alcohol is served. Is it now time to re-think the ban on smoking in public places? Since the needs and desires of all people need to be considered in a democratic society, it may be time to re-evaluate this restriction.

Perspective 1

The ban on cigarette smoking in public places should be repealed as it is yet another example of too much governmental regulation in our daily lives. Those who do not like smoking can simply go somewhere else to eat or drink.

Perspective 2

The ban on cigarette smoking should actually be extended to all states and should include more venues, such as casinos. Many people die needlessly every year due to the effects of second-hand smoking.

Perspective 3

The ban on cigarette smoking appears to have been working well for years in the states that have adopted these laws. There is really no need to change the status quo since current regulations are effective.

ACT Essay Prompt 15

Those in the sports and entertainment industries can be said to serve noble purposes in keeping us entertained, especially during the hard times of life. Some would therefore argue that sports stars and actors are deserving of the large salaries that they are paid. On the other hand, others point out that athletes and other celebrities earn far more than those performing socially essential jobs, such as education and law enforcement. Are athletes and entertainers paid too much? Since being fairly compensated for work is a basic human right, a discussion of this topic is worthwhile.

Perspective 1

Athletes and actors serve no useful purpose in society whatsoever. The salaries that they are paid should be highly taxed so that more public funds could be allocated to pay those in socially-necessary jobs.

Perspective 2

After a hard week at work, nothing is better than watching a game or a movie. Athletes and entertainers do merit the pay they earn because they help to cheer us up and bring fun and laughter to our lives.

Perspective 3

While some athletes are entertainers appear to be highly paid, their careers are sometimes cut short, especially by aging or injury. They also spend more money, which helps out the local and national economies.

ACT Essay Prompt 16

The census has revealed that many families regularly overspend. However, some families could not live day to day without going into debt. Credit card companies are sometimes only too happy to offer more credit to consumers that are already in financial trouble. Who is to blame in this situation: consumers, credit card companies, or something else? Levels of personal debt are constantly increasing, so this compelling question requires our attention.

Perspective 1

Only one person is to blame when credit card balances are out of control: the consumer. Financial companies cannot confer self-control on others, nor can they control consumers, who will simply go elsewhere to get credit.

Perspective 2

Credit card companies and financial institutions are culpable for thousands of personal-bankruptcy claims each year. The government should do more to regulate the amount of credit that companies can extend to consumers in trouble.

Perspective 3

Certain controls on the credit card industry need to be re-evaluated, especially the amount of fees and the rate of interest that they can charge. However, spending is a matter of personal choice, so no limits should be placed on credit card balances.

Appendix – Grammar and Punctuation Review

Mechanical conventions are the rules of grammar and punctuation that are necessary in order to write accurately and correctly.

This section is intended as a basic overview of some of the most important mechanical conventions for the exam.

Comparatives and Superlatives – Avoid Using Double Forms:

Use the comparative form when comparing two things.

The comparative form consists of the adjective plus –er when the adjective has two syllables or less.

pretty → prettier

Avoid making a double comparative:

INCORRECT: more prettier

When the adjective has more than two syllables, the adjective should be preceded by the word "more" in order to form the comparative.

beautiful → more beautiful

Examples:

Tom is taller than his brother.

Tom is more intelligent than his brother.

If you are comparing more than two things, you must use the superlative form.

As a general rule, the superlative form consists of the adjective plus –est when the adjective has two syllables or less.

pretty → prettiest

Avoid making a double superlative:

INCORRECT: most prettiest

To form the superlative for adjectives that have more than two syllables, the adjective should be preceded by the word "most".

beautiful → most beautiful

Examples:

Tom is the tallest boy in his class.

Tom is the most intelligent boy in his class.

Correct Use of *Its* and *It's*:

"Its" is a possessive pronoun, while "it's" is a contraction of "it is."

CORRECT: It's high time you started to study.

INCORRECT: Its high time you started to study.

The sentence could also be stated as follows: It is high time that you started to study.

Since the contracted form of "it is" is used in the alternative sentence, "it's" is the correct form.

CORRECT: A snake sheds its skin at least once a year.

INCORRECT: A snake sheds it's skin at least once a year.

"Its" is a possessive pronoun referring to the snake, so the apostrophe should not be used.

Correct Use of *Their*, *There*, and *They're*:

"Their" is a plural possessive pronoun.

"There" is used to describe the location of something.

"They're" is a contraction of "they are."

CORRECT: Their house is made of brick and concrete.

INCORRECT: There house is made of brick and concrete.

INCORRECT: They're house is made of brick and concrete.

In this case, "their" is the possessive pronoun explaining to whom the house belongs.

CORRECT: He attended college with his cousins living there in California.

INCORRECT: He attended college with his cousins living their in California.

INCORRECT: He attended college with his cousins living they're in California.

"There" is referring to the state of California in the example above, so it is used to talk about the location.

CORRECT: They're away on vacation at the moment.

INCORRECT: Their away on vacation at the moment.

INCORRECT: There away on vacation at the moment.

The sentence could also be written as follows: They are away on vacation at the moment.

"They're" is a contraction of "they are," so the apostrophe needs to be used.

Correct Use of *Were*, *Where*, and *We're*:

"Were" is the past tense of the verb "are."

"Where" is used to inquire about or describe the location of something.

"We're" is a contraction of "we are."

CORRECT: They were going to call you, but the phone was out of order.

INCORRECT: They where going to call you, but the phone was out of order.

INCORRECT: They we're going to call you, but the phone was out of order.

"Were" is the past form of the verb in the sentence above.

CORRECT: Where is the mall located?

INCORRECT: Were is the mall located?

INCORRECT: We're is the mall located?

"Where" needs to be used because the sentence is making an inquiry about the location of the mall.

CORRECT: We're so happy that you got accepted into college.

INCORRECT: Were so happy that you got accepted into college.

INCORRECT: Where so happy that you got accepted into college.

The sentence could be written as follows: We are so happy that you got accepted into college.

"We're" is a contraction of "we are," so the apostrophe needs to be used.

Avoid the "is where" construction:

CORRECT: An identity crisis, which is the experience of confusion about one's life goals and ambitions, often occurs in middle age.

INCORRECT: An identity crisis is where there is the experience of confusion about one's life goals and ambitions, and it often occurs in middle age.

The construction in the second sentence may be used in informal speaking, but such constructions should be avoided in your essay.

Misplaced Modifiers:

Modifiers are phrases that describe other parts of a sentence. The modifier should always be placed directly before or after the noun to which it relates.

Now look at these examples:

CORRECT: Like Minnesota, Wisconsin gets extremely cold in the winter.

INCORRECT: Like Minnesota, it gets extremely cold in Wisconsin in the winter.

The phrase "like Minnesota" is an adjectival phrase that modifies the noun "Wisconsin."

Therefore, "Wisconsin" must come directly after the comma.

Here are two more examples:

CORRECT: While at the mall, a gang of youths committed a robbery.

INCORRECT: While at the mall, a robbery was committed.

The adverbial phrase "while at the mall" modifies the noun phrase "a gang of youths," so this noun phrase needs to come after the adverbial phrase.

Parallelism:

When giving items in a series, be sure to use consistent forms.

CORRECT: The position involves answering phone calls, writing letters, and getting supplies.

INCORRECT: The position involves answering phone calls, writing letters, and get supplies.

All of the items in the series should be in the –ing form.

CORRECT: I saw Tom's accident yesterday, and I tried to help.

INCORRECT: I saw Tom's accident yesterday, and I try to help.

Both parts of the sentence are describing actions that occurred yesterday, so the past tense needs to be used for both verbs.

Punctuation and Independent Clauses – Avoiding Run-On Sentences:

Run-on sentences are those that use commas to join independent clauses together, instead of correctly using the period.

An independent clause contains a grammatical subject and verb. It therefore can stand alone as its own sentence.

The first word of the independent clause should begin with a capital letter, and the clause should be preceded by a period.

CORRECT: I thought I would live in this city forever. Then I lost my job.

INCORRECT: I thought I would live in this city forever, then I lost my job.

"Then I lost my job" is a complete sentence. It has a grammatical subject (I) and a verb (lost). The independent clause must be preceded by a period, and the first word of the new sentence must begin with a capital letter.

Alternatively, an appropriate conjunction can be used to join the independent clauses:

I thought I would live in this city forever, and then I lost my job.

Punctuation and Quotation Marks:

Punctuation should be enclosed within the final quotation mark when giving dialogue.

CORRECT: "I can't believe you bought a new car," Sam remarked.

INCORRECT: "I can't believe you bought a new car", Sam remarked.

In the example below, the word "exclaimed" shows that the exclamation point is needed.

CORRECT: "I can't believe you bought a new car!" Sam exclaimed.

INCORRECT: "I can't believe you bought a new car"! Sam exclaimed.

However, if the quotation is stated indirectly, no quotation marks should be used.

CORRECT: Sam exclaimed that he couldn't believe that I had bought a new car.

INCORRECT: Sam exclaimed that "he couldn't believe that I had bought a new car."

Punctuation for Items in a Series:

When using "and" and "or" for more than two items in a series, be sure to use the comma before the words "and" and "or."

CORRECT: You need to bring a tent, sleeping bag, and flashlight.

INCORRECT: You need to bring a tent, sleeping bag and flashlight.

Notice the use of the comma after the word "bag" and before the word "and" in the series.

CORRECT: Students can call, write a letter, or send an email.

INCORRECT: Students can call, write a letter or send an email.

Notice the use of the comma after the word "letter" and before the word "or" in the series.

Restrictive and Non-restrictive Modifiers:

Restrictive modifiers are clauses or phrases that provide essential information in order to identify the grammatical subject. Restrictive modifiers should not be preceded by a comma.

Example: My sister who lives in Indianapolis is a good swimmer.

In this case, the speaker has more than one sister, and she is identifying which sister she is talking about by giving the essential information "who lives in Indianapolis."

On the other hand, a non-restrictive modifier is a clause or phrase that provides extra information about a grammatical subject in a sentence. A non-restrictive modifier must be preceded by a comma.

Non-restrictive modifiers are also known as non-essential modifiers.

Example: My sister, who lives in Indianapolis, is a good swimmer.

In this case, the speaker has only one sister. Therefore, the information about her sister's city of residence is not essential in order to identify which sister she is talking about.

The words "who lives in Indianapolis" form a non-restrictive modifier.

Sentence Fragments:

A sentence fragment is a group of words that does not express a complete train of thought.

CORRECT: I like Denver because it has a great university.

INCORRECT: I like Denver. Because it has a great university.

In the second example, "because it has a great university" is not a complete thought. This idea needs to be joined with the previous clause in order to be grammatically correct.

Subject-Verb Agreement:

Subjects must agree with verbs in number.

Subject-verb agreement can be confusing when there are intervening words in a sentence.

CORRECT: The flowers in the pot in the garden grow quickly.

INCORRECT: The flowers in the pot in the garden grows quickly.

The grammatical subject in the above sentence is "flowers," not "pot" or "garden," so the plural form of the verb (*grow*) needs to be used.

CORRECT: Each person in the groups of students needs to pay attention to the instructions.

INCORRECT: Each person in the groups of students need to pay attention to the instructions.

The grammatical subject in the above sentence is "each person," not "students." "Each" is singular and therefore needs the singular form of the verb (*needs*).

Using Correct Grammar and Punctuation – Exercises

Each of the sentences below has problems with grammar and punctuation. Find the errors in the sentences and correct them. You may wish to refer to the advice in the previous section as you do the exercise.

The answers are provided on the page following the exercises.

1) I haven't seen her or her sister. Since they went away to college.

2) People who like to get up early in the morning in order to drink more coffee is likely to become easily tired in the afternoon.

3) Were we're you when we called you yesterday?

4) She is the most happiest person that I know.

5) Hanging from the knob on the bedroom door, Tom thought the new shirt was his favorite.

6) I ran across the street to speak to her, then she surprised me by saying "that she had bought a new car."

7) Its common for a magazine to have better sales if it mentions computers, handhelds or other new technology on it's cover.

8) After losing long-term employment, many people suffer from anxiety, loneliness and get depressed.

9) Each student in the class who will take the series of exams on advanced mathematics need to study in advance.

10) Their are several reasons why there having problems with they're children.

Using Correct Grammar and Punctuation – Answers

1) I haven't seen her or her sister since they went away to college.

2) People who like to get up early in the morning in order to drink more coffee are likely to become easily tired in the afternoon.

3) Where were you when we called you yesterday?

4) She is the happiest person that I know.

5) Hanging from the knob on the bedroom door, the new shirt was Tom's favorite.

6) I ran across the street to speak to her. Then she surprised me by saying that she had bought a new car.

7) It's common for a magazine to have better sales if it mentions computers, handhelds, or other new technology on its cover.

8) After losing long-term employment, many people suffer from anxiety, loneliness, and depression.

9) Each student in the class who will take the series of exams on advanced mathematics needs to study in advance.

10) There are several reasons why they're having problems with their children.

Vocabulary for the ACT Essay – Using the Academic Word List

This study guide has covered the various aspects of grammar and structure that you need to demonstrate in your essay.

However, the examiner also assesses your vocabulary level as he or she reads through the various paragraphs of your essay.

The following pages contain a list of academic words. You should study the list and try to use these words in your ACT essay.

Academic Word List

abundant	argue
acceptability	aspect
acceptable	atrocity
access	attribute
accessibility	believe
accessible	capacity
accumulate	catalyst
accurate	category
acknowledge	caveat
acquire	circumstance
admit	cite
adversity	claim
advocate	clarify
affirm	codify
aggregate	coherent
agitate	comment
agitation	communicate
analogy	compile
announce	compose
approbation	comprehensive
appropriate	conclude
approve	concurrent
arguably	conduct

confirm	derive
consider	deviate
consist	differentiate
constitute	diminish
construct	discern
consult	discipline
contemplate	discriminate
contradict	dispose
contravene	dispute
controversy	distribute
convenient	diverse
convention	document
conventional	dominate
convey	drawback
create	eliminate
credence	emerge
criteria	emphasize
crucial	empirical
decline	encounter
deduce	enforce
demonstrate	enhance
deny	enumerate
despotic	environment
determine	equate
deterrent	equivalent

erode	gratify
establish	guideline
estimate	heinous
evaluate	hierarchy
evident	highlight
exhibit	hypothesis
exist	identify
existence	ideology
experience	illustrate
explicit	immense
exploit	impact
extract	implement
facilitate	implicate
factor	imply
feature	inappropriate
fluctuate	incentive
focus	incidence
formula	indicate
foundation	individual
framework	induce
fundamental	inevitable
general	infer
generate	inflection
grant	inhabitant
gratification	inherent

innovate	labor
input	legislate
insidious	levy
insight	liberal
inspect	literal
instance	locate
instruct	logic
integral	maintain
integrity	major
intense	manipulate
interact	maximize
interpret	mechanism
intervene	media
intrinsic	mediate
investigate	method
invoke	minimize
involve	misconstrue
ironically	misfortune
irretrievable	misinterpret
isolate	mode
issue	modify
item	motive
judgment	mutual
justify	negate
	network

neutral

norm

notion

nuance

objective

observe

obtain

occasion

occupy

occur

offender

offset

ongoing

option

outcome

oversee

paradigm

parallel

parameter

participate

perceive

persecute

perspective

phenomenon

philosophy

policy

possession

postulate

potential

precede

precise

predict

predominant

preliminary

presume

previous

primary

principal

priority

process

professional

prohibit

promote

proportion

propose

prospect

protocol

publication

purchase

pursue	restrain
quote	restrict
rational	restriction
recipient	reveal
recover	revenue
refine	reverse
refute	revise
regime	satisfaction
register	satisfy
regrettable	scenario
regulate	schadenfreude
reinforce	scheme
reject	scope
release	select
relevant	sequence
reluctant	shortcoming
remarkable	significant
repudiate	situation
require	specific
research	specify
reside	statistic
resolve	status
resource	stipulate
respond	straightforward
restore	strategy

stricken
structure
submit
subordinate
subsequent
subtlety
sufficient
summary
supplement
surrender
survey
suspend
sustain
technique
technology
terminate
theory
transform
ultimate
ultimatum
undergo
underlie
undertake
unfortunate
uniform

unimaginable
unique
unthinkable
untoward
utilize
utter
utterance
valid
vary
version
widespread
would-be
wrongdoing

NOTES: